1999 CASE AND STATUTORY SUPPLEMENT

EMPLOYMENT DISCRIMINATION LAW

CASES AND MATERIALS

Second Edition

By

Mack A. Player
Dean and Professor
Santa Clara University
School of Law

Elaine W. Shoben
Edward W. Cleary Professor
University of Illinois
College of Law

AMERICAN CASEBOOK SERIES®

WEST GROUP

ST. PAUL, MINN., 1999

American Casebook Series, and the West Group
symbol are used herein under license.

COPYRIGHT © 1999 By WEST GROUP
                        610 Opperman Drive
                        P.O. Box 64526
                        St. Paul, MN 55164–0526
                        1–800–328–9352

ISBN 0–314–23964–2

 *TEXT IS PRINTED ON 10% POST
CONSUMER RECYCLED PAPER*

Preface

This book accompanies the Player, Shoben & Lieberwitz casebook on *Employment Discrimination*, second edition. It contains both the textual additions and the statutory supplement in one unit for the convenience of the user.

The major developments in employment discrimination law since the publication of the second edition have come from the Supreme Court in two areas. In the 1997–98 Term, the Court decided several Title VII sexual harassment cases that have dramatically changed the litigation in this area, particularly with respect to the basis for employer liability. Then in the 1998–99 Term, the Court decided several major cases under the Americans with Disabilities Act, notably erecting a higher threshold for coverage under that Act. This Supplement presents these cases as well as noting other important developments in the areas of sovereign immunity, gay rights, mandatory arbitration, and punitive damages.

The second part of this Supplement contains excerpts from the federal statutes relevant to the text, including the major antidiscrimination statutes and related matters, such as fee recovery. The statutory supplement is substantially unchanged from prior editions, but note that the Civil Rights Act of 1991 is no longer included as a separate act. It is incorporated in the acts that it amends.

This unified supplement should be a useful tool for guiding students through the increasingly complex area of employment discrimination law. It is designed to permit continual rooting in the statutory texts as well as to provide a convenient up-date in this ever-changing field.

MACK A. PLAYER
Dean and Professor
Santa Clara University School of Law

ELAINE W. SHOBEN
Edward W. Cleary Professor
University of Illinois College of Law

*

Table of Contents

PART VII.   PROCEDURES AND REMEDIES

Table of Cases

The principal cases are in bold type. Cases cited or discussed in the text are roman type. References are to pages. Cases cited in principal cases and within other quoted materials are not included.

*

*

1999 CASE AND STATUTORY SUPPLEMENT

EMPLOYMENT DISCRIMINATION LAW

CASES AND MATERIALS

Second Edition

*

Part I

INTRODUCTION

Chapter 3

"RANGE" OF THE MAJOR STATUTES: COVERAGE AND SCOPE

A. TITLE VII, THE AMERICANS WITH DISABILITIES ACT, AND THE AGE DISCRIMINATION IN EMPLOYMENT ACT

1. "EMPLOYER"—COVERAGE

Page 50: "Fifteen or More Employees"

The question raised in the text of how to count employees for the purpose of coverage was resolved by *Walters v. Metropolitan Educational Enterprises,* 519 U.S. 202, 117 S.Ct. 660, 136 L.Ed.2d 644 (1997). The employer maintained fifteen or more employees on the payroll for the requisite number of weeks. However, fewer than fifteen employees might report to work on each day of the calendar week. The employer argued that those weeks could not be counted for the purpose of determining "employer" coverage. The Seventh Circuit accepted the argument of the employer "that if asked how many employees he had for a given working day, he would give as the answer the number of employees who were *actually performing work on that day*," rather than the number of employees "on the payroll." A unanimous Supreme Court reversed, concluding: "Such a disposition is so improbable and so impossible to administer (few employers keep daily attendance records of all their salaried employees) that Congress should be thought to have prescribed it only if the language could bear no other meaning."

Special Types of "Employers"

Page 53–54: State and Local Governments

Seminole Tribe v. Florida, 517 U.S. 44, 116 S.Ct. 1114, 134 L.Ed.2d 252 (1996) held that Congress does not have the power under the "Indian Commerce Clause" to abrogate state sovereignty guaranteed by the Eleventh Amendment. This revitalizes the constitutional questions concerning age and disability discrimination cases brought by individuals

2

against a state employer in federal courts. For example, *MacPherson v. University of Montevallo*, 938 F.Supp. 785 (N.D.Ala. 1996) held that Congress does not have power under the ADEA to abrogate state sovereign immunity in that the ADEA is an exercise of Congressional power under the "commerce clause" rather than the Fourteenth Amendment, and that states are protected by the sovereign immunity granted by the Eleventh Amendment against ADEA suits. (Note: the Fourteenth Amendment authority for enacting race, sex, religious and national origin discrimination legislation continues to justify private suits against state employers under Title VII).

*

Part II

"DISCRIMINATION": PRINCIPLES AND PROOF

Chapter 6

IMPROPER MOTIVATION

A. INDIVIDUAL DISCRIMINATION

2. CIRCUMSTANTIAL EVIDENCE OF DISCRIMINATION

Page 193—204: At 204 Improper Motivation

O'CONNOR v. CONSOLIDATED COIN CATERERS CORP.

Supreme Court of the United States, 1996.
517 U.S. 308, 116 S.Ct. 1307, 134 L.Ed.2d 433.

JUSTICE SCALIA delivered the opinion of the Court.

This case presents the question whether a plaintiff alleging that he was discharged in violation of the Age Discrimination in Employment Act of 1967 (ADEA), must show that he was replaced by someone outside the age group protected by the ADEA to make out a prima facie case under the framework established by McDonnell Douglas Corp. v. Green, 411 U.S. 792, 93 S.Ct. 1817, 36 L.Ed.2d 668 (1973).

Petitioner James O'Connor was employed by respondent Consolidated Coin Caterers Corporation from 1978 until August 10, 1990, when, at age 56, he was fired. Claiming that he had been dismissed because of his age in violation of the ADEA, petitioner brought suit in the United States District Court for the Western District of North Carolina. After discovery, the District Court granted respondent's motion for summary judgment,and petitioner appealed. The Court of Appeals for the Fourth Circuit stated that petitioner could establish a prima facie case under McDonnell Douglas only if he could prove that (1) he was in the age group protected by the ADEA; (2) he was discharged or demoted; (3) at the time of his discharge or demotion, he was performing his job at a level that met his employer's legitimate expectations; and (4) following his discharge or demotion, he was replaced by someone of comparable qualifications outside the protected class. Since petitioner's replacement was 40 years old, the Court of Appeals concluded that the last element of the prima facie case had not been made out. * * *

6

* * * [T]he question presented for our determination is what elements must be shown in an ADEA case to establish the prima facie case that triggers the employer's burden of production.

As the very name "prima facie case" suggests, there must be at least a logical connection between each element of the prima facie case and the illegal discrimination for which it establishes a "legally mandatory, rebuttable presumption. The element of replacement by someone under 40 fails this requirement." The discrimination prohibited by the ADEA is discrimination "because of [an] individual's age," though the prohibition is "limited to individuals who are at least 40 years of age." This language does not ban discrimination against employees because they are aged 40 or older; it bans discrimination against employees because of their age, but limits the protected class to those who are 40 or older. The fact that one person in the protected class has lost out to another person in the protected class is thus irrelevant, so long as he has lost out because of his age. Or to put the point more concretely, there can be no greater inference of age discrimination (as opposed to "40 or over" discrimination) when a 40 year-old is replaced by a 39 year-old than when a 56 year-old is replaced by a 40 year-old. Because it lacks probative value, the fact that an ADEA plaintiff was replaced by someone outside the protected class is not a proper element of the McDonnell Douglas prima facie case.

Perhaps some courts have been induced to adopt the principle urged by respondent in order to avoid creating a prima facie case on the basis of very thin evidence—for example, the replacement of a 68 year-old by a 65 year-old. While the respondent's principle theoretically permits such thin evidence (consider the example above of a 40 year-old replaced by a 39 year-old), as a practical matter it will rarely do so, since the vast majority of age-discrimination claims come from older employees. In our view, however, the proper solution to the problem lies not in making an utterly irrelevant factor an element of the prima facie case, but rather in recognizing that the prima facie case requires "evidence adequate to create an inference that an employment decision was based on a[n] [illegal] discriminatory criterion. ... " In the age-discrimination context, such an inference can not be drawn from the replacement of one worker with another worker insignificantly younger. Because the ADEA prohibits discrimination on the basis of age and not class membership, the fact that a replacement is substantially younger than the plaintiff is a far more reliable indicator of age discrimination than is the fact that the plaintiff was replaced by someone outside the protected class.

The judgment of the Fourth Circuit is reversed, and the case is remanded for proceedings consistent with this opinion.

It is so ordered.

*

Part III

CONDITIONS OF EMPLOYMENT

Chapter 11

HARASSMENT

B. SEXUAL HARASSMENT

Page 382: Replace *Stacks* and Notes 1 and 2 following it with:

BURLINGTON INDUSTRIES, INC. v. ELLERTH

Supreme Court of the United States, 1998.
524 U.S. 742, 118 S.Ct. 2257, 141 L.Ed.2d 633.

JUSTICE KENNEDY delivered the opinion of the Court.

We decide whether, under Title VII of the Civil Rights Act of 1964 an employee who refuses the unwelcome and threatening sexual advances of a supervisor, yet suffers no adverse, tangible job consequences, can recover against the employer without showing the employer is negligent or otherwise at fault for the supervisor's actions.

I

Summary judgment was granted for the employer, so we must take the facts alleged by the employee to be true. [Citation.] The employer is Burlington Industries, the petitioner. The employee is Kimberly Ellerth, the respondent. From March 1993 until May 1994, Ellerth worked as a salesperson in one of Burlington's divisions in Chicago, Illinois. During her employment, she alleges, she was subjected to constant sexual harassment by her supervisor, one Ted Slowik.

In the hierarchy of Burlington's management structure, Slowik was a mid-level manager. Burlington has eight divisions, employing more than 22,000 people in some 50 plants around the United States. Slowik was a vice president in one of five business units within one of the divisions. He had authority to make hiring and promotion decisions subject to the approval of his supervisor, who signed the paperwork. According to Slowik's supervisor, his position was "not considered an upper-level management position," and he was "not amongst the decision-making or policy-making hierarchy." Slowik was not Ellerth's immediate supervisor. Ellerth worked in a two-person office in Chicago,

10

and she answered to her office colleague, who in turn answered to Slowik in New York.

Against a background of repeated boorish and offensive remarks and gestures which Slowik allegedly made, Ellerth places particular emphasis on three alleged incidents where Slowik's comments could be construed as threats to deny her tangible job benefits. In the summer of 1993, while on a business trip, Slowik invited Ellerth to the hotel lounge, an invitation Ellerth felt compelled to accept because Slowik was her boss. When Ellerth gave no encouragement to remarks Slowik made about her breasts, he told her to "loosen up" and warned, "[y]ou know, Kim, I could make your life very hard or very easy at Burlington."

In March 1994, when Ellerth was being considered for a promotion, Slowik expressed reservations during the promotion interview because she was not "loose enough." The comment was followed by his reaching over and rubbing her knee. Ellerth did receive the promotion; but when Slowik called to announce it, he told Ellerth, "you're gonna be out there with men who work in factories, and they certainly like women with pretty butts/legs."

In May 1994, Ellerth called Slowik, asking permission to insert a customer's logo into a fabric sample. Slowik responded, "I don't have time for you right now, Kim—unless you want to tell me what you're wearing." Ellerth told Slowik she had to go and ended the call. A day or two later, Ellerth called Slowik to ask permission again. This time he denied her request, but added something along the lines of, "are you wearing shorter skirts yet, Kim, because it would make your job a whole heck of a lot easier."

A short time later, Ellerth's immediate supervisor cautioned her about returning telephone calls to customers in a prompt fashion. In response, Ellerth quit. She faxed a letter giving reasons unrelated to the alleged sexual harassment we have described. About three weeks later, however, she sent a letter explaining she quit because of Slowik's behavior.

During her tenure at Burlington, Ellerth did not inform anyone in authority about Slowik's conduct, despite knowing Burlington had a policy against sexual harassment. In fact, she chose not to inform her immediate supervisor (not Slowik) because " 'it would be his duty as my supervisor to report any incidents of sexual harassment.' " On one occasion, she told Slowik a comment he made was inappropriate. * * *

II

At the outset, we assume an important proposition yet to be established before a trier of fact. It is a premise assumed as well, in explicit or implicit terms, in the various opinions by the judges of the Court of Appeals. The premise is: a trier of fact could find in Slowik's remarks numerous threats to retaliate against Ellerth if she denied some sexual liberties. The threats, however, were not carried out or fulfilled. Cases based on threats which are carried out are referred to often as quid pro quo cases, as distinct from bothersome attentions or sexual remarks that are sufficiently severe or pervasive to create a hostile work environment. The terms quid pro quo and hostile work environment are helpful, perhaps, in making a rough demarcation between cases in which threats are carried out and those where they are not or are absent altogether, but beyond this are of limited utility.

* * *

We do not suggest the terms quid pro quo and hostile work environment are irrelevant to Title VII litigation. To the extent they illustrate the distinction between cases involving a threat which is carried out and offensive conduct in general, the terms are relevant when there is a threshold question whether a plaintiff can prove discrimination in violation of Title VII. When a plaintiff proves that a tangible employment action resulted from a refusal to submit to a supervisor's sexual demands, he or she establishes that the employment decision itself constitutes a change in the terms and conditions of employment that is actionable under Title VII. For any sexual harassment preceding the employment decision to be actionable, however, the conduct must be severe or pervasive. Because Ellerth's claim involves only unfulfilled threats, it should be categorized as a hostile work environment claim which requires a showing of severe or pervasive conduct. [Citations.] For purposes of this case, we accept the District Court's finding that the alleged conduct was severe or pervasive. The case before us involves numerous alleged threats, and we express no opinion as to whether a single unfulfilled threat is sufficient to constitute discrimination in the terms or conditions of employment.

When we assume discrimination can be proved, however, the factors we discuss below, and not the categories quid pro quo and hostile work environment, will be controlling on the issue of vicarious liability. That is the question we must resolve.

III

We must decide, then, whether an employer has vicarious liability when a supervisor creates a hostile work environment by making explicit threats to alter a subordinate's terms or conditions of employment, based on sex, but does not fulfill the threat. We turn to principles of agency law, for the term "employer" is defined under Title VII to include "agents." 42 U.S.C. § 2000e(b); see Meritor, supra, at 72, 106 S.Ct., at 2408–2409. In express terms, Congress has directed federal courts to interpret Title VII based on agency principles. Given such an explicit instruction, we conclude a uniform and predictable standard must be established as a matter of federal law. * * *

Section 219(1) of the Restatement sets out a central principle of agency law:

"A master is subject to liability for the torts of his servants committed while acting in the scope of their employment."

An employer may be liable for both negligent and intentional torts committed by an employee within the scope of his or her employment. Sexual harassment under Title VII presupposes intentional conduct. * * * The Restatement defines conduct, including an intentional tort, to be within the scope of employment when "actuated, at least in part, by a purpose to serve the [employer]," even if it is forbidden by the employer. Restatement §§ 228(1)(c), 230. For example, when a salesperson lies to a customer to make a sale, the tortious conduct is within the scope of employment because it benefits the employer by increasing sales, even though it may violate the employer's policies. See Prosser and Keeton on Torts § 70, at 505–506.

As Courts of Appeals have recognized, a supervisor acting out of gender-based animus or a desire to fulfill sexual urges may not be actuated by a purpose to serve the employer. [Citations.] The harassing supervisor often acts for personal motives, motives unrelated and even antithetical to the objectives of the employer. [Citations.] There are instances, of course, where a supervisor engages in unlawful discrimination with the purpose, mistaken or otherwise, to serve the employer. E.g., Sims v. Montgomery County Comm'n, 766 F.Supp. 1052, 1075 (M.D.Ala.1990) (supervisor acting in scope of employment where employer has a policy of discouraging women from seeking advancement and "sexual harassment was simply a way of furthering that policy").

* * *

The general rule is that sexual harassment by a supervisor is not conduct within the scope of employment. * * * [But scope of employment] does not define the only basis for employer liability under agency principles. In limited circumstances, agency principles impose liability on employers even where employees commit torts outside the scope of employment. The principles are set forth in the much-cited § 219(2) of the Restatement:

"(2) A master is not subject to liability for the torts of his servants acting outside the scope of their employment, unless:

"(a) the master intended the conduct or the consequences, or

"(b) the master was negligent or reckless, or

"(c) the conduct violated a non-delegable duty of the master, or

"(d) the servant purported to act or to speak on behalf of the principal and there was reliance upon apparent authority, or he was aided in accomplishing the tort by the existence of the agency relation."

* * * Subsections (b) and (d) are possible grounds for imposing employer liability on account of a supervisor's acts and must be considered. Under subsection (b), an employer is liable when the tort is attributable to the employer's own negligence. § 219(2)(b). Thus, although a supervisor's sexual harassment is outside the scope of employment because the conduct was for personal motives, an employer can be

liable, nonetheless, where its own negligence is a cause of the harassment. An employer is negligent with respect to sexual harassment if it knew or should have known about the conduct and failed to stop it. Negligence sets a minimum standard for employer liability under Title VII; but Ellerth seeks to invoke the more stringent standard of vicarious liability.

Subsection 219(2)(d) concerns vicarious liability for intentional torts committed by an employee when the employee uses apparent authority (the apparent authority standard), or when the employee "was aided in accomplishing the tort by the existence of the agency relation" (the aided in the agency relation standard). * * *

As a general rule, apparent authority is relevant where the agent purports to exercise a power which he or she does not have, as distinct from where the agent threatens to misuse actual power. Compare Restatement § 6 (defining "power") with § 8 (defining "apparent authority"). In the usual case, a supervisor's harassment involves misuse of actual power, not the false impression of its existence. Apparent authority analysis therefore is inappropriate in this context. If, in the unusual case, it is alleged there is a false impression that the actor was a supervisor, when he in fact was not, the victim's mistaken conclusion must be a reasonable one. Restatement § 8, Comment c ("Apparent authority exists only to the extent it is reasonable for the third person dealing with the agent to believe that the agent is authorized"). When a party seeks to impose vicarious liability based on an agent's misuse of delegated authority, the Restatement's aided in the agency relation rule, rather than the apparent authority rule, appears to be the appropriate form of analysis.

We turn to the aided in the agency relation standard. In a sense, most workplace tortfeasors are aided in accomplishing their tortious objective by the existence of the agency relation: Proximity and regular contact may afford a captive pool of potential victims. [Citation.] Were this to satisfy the aided in the agency relation standard, an employer would be subject to vicarious liability not only for all supervisor harassment, but also for all co-worker harassment, a result enforced by neither the EEOC nor any court of appeals to have considered the issue. [Citations.] The aided in the agency relation standard, therefore, requires the existence of something more than the employment relation itself.

At the outset, we can identify a class of cases where, beyond question, more than the mere existence of the employment relation aids in commission of the harassment: when a supervisor takes a tangible employment action against the subordinate. * * * Although few courts have elaborated how agency principles support this rule, we think it reflects a correct application of the aided in the agency relation standard.

In the context of this case, a tangible employment action would have taken the form of a denial of a raise or a promotion. * * * When a supervisor makes a tangible employment decision, there is assurance the injury could not have been inflicted absent the agency relation. A tangible employment action in most cases inflicts direct economic harm. As a general proposition, only a supervisor, or other person acting with the authority of the company, can cause this sort of injury. A co-worker can break a co-worker's arm as easily as a supervisor, and anyone who has regular contact with an employee can inflict psychological injuries by his or her offensive conduct. [Citation.] But one co-worker (absent some elaborate scheme) cannot dock another's pay, nor can one co-worker demote another. Tangible employment actions fall within the special province of the supervisor. The supervisor has been empowered by the company as a distinct class of agent to make economic decisions affecting other employees under his or her control.

* * *

Whether the agency relation aids in commission of supervisor harassment which does not culminate in a tangible employment action is less obvious. Application of the standard is made difficult by its malleable terminology, which can be read to either expand or limit liability in the context of supervisor harassment. On the one hand, a supervisor's power and authority invests his or her harassing conduct with a particular threatening character, and in this sense, a supervisor always is aided by the agency relation. [Citation.] On the other hand, there are acts of harassment a supervisor might commit which might be the same acts a co-employee would commit, and there may be some circumstances where the supervisor's status makes little difference.

* * *

In order to accommodate the agency principles of vicarious liability for harm caused by misuse of supervisory authority, as well as Title VII's equally basic policies of encouraging forethought by employers and saving action by objecting employees, we adopt the following holding in this case and in Faragher v. Boca Raton, also decided today. An employer is subject to vicarious liability to a victimized employee for an actionable hostile environment created by a supervisor with immediate (or successively higher) authority over the employee. When no tangible employment action is taken, a defending employer may raise an affirmative defense to liability or damages, subject to proof by a preponderance of the evidence, see Fed. Rule Civ. Proc. 8(c). The defense comprises two necessary elements: (a) that the employer exercised reasonable care to prevent and correct promptly any sexually harassing behavior, and (b) that the plaintiff employee unreasonably failed to take advantage of any preventive or corrective opportunities provided by the employer or to avoid harm otherwise. While proof that an employer had promulgated an anti-harassment policy with complaint procedure is not necessary in every instance as a matter of law, the need for a stated policy suitable to the employment circumstances may appropriately be addressed in any case when litigating the first element of the defense. And while proof that an employee failed to fulfill the corresponding obligation of reasonable care to avoid harm is not limited to showing any unreasonable failure to use any complaint procedure provided by the employer, a demonstration of such failure will normally suffice to satisfy the employer's burden under the second element of the defense. No affirmative defense is available, however, when the supervisor's harassment culminates in a tangible employment action, such as discharge, demotion, or undesirable reassignment.

IV

Relying on existing case law which held out the promise of vicarious liability for all quid pro quo claims, Ellerth focused all her attention in the Court of Appeals on proving her claim fit within that category. Given our explanation that the labels quid pro quo and hostile work environment are not controlling for purposes of establishing employer liability, Ellerth should have an adequate opportunity to prove she has a claim for which Burlington is liable.

* * *

It is so ordered.

JUSTICE THOMAS, with whom JUSTICE SCALIA joins, dissenting.

The Court today manufactures a rule that employers are vicariously liable if supervisors create a sexually hostile work environment, subject to an affirmative defense that the Court barely attempts to define. This rule applies even if the employer has a policy against sexual harassment, the employee knows about that policy, and the employee never informs anyone in a position of authority about the supervisor's conduct. As a result, employer liability under Title VII is judged by different standards depending upon whether a sexually or racially hostile work environment is alleged. The standard of employer liability should be the same in both instances: An employer should be liable if, and only if, the plaintiff proves that the employer was negligent in permitting the supervisor's conduct to occur.

* * *

Page 388: Insert after Notes:

FARAGHER v. CITY OF BOCA RATON

Supreme Court of the United States, 1998.
524 U.S. 775, 118 S.Ct. 2275, 141 L.Ed.2d 662.

JUSTICE SOUTER delivered the opinion of the Court.

This case calls for identification of the circumstances under which an employer may be held liable under Title VII of the Civil Rights Act of 1964 for the acts of a supervisory employee whose sexual harassment of subordinates has created a hostile work environment amounting to employment discrimination. We hold that an employer is vicariously liable for actionable discrimination caused by a supervisor, but subject to an affirmative defense looking to the reasonableness of the employer's conduct as well as that of a plaintiff victim.

Between 1985 and 1990, while attending college, petitioner Beth Ann Faragher worked part time and during the summers as an ocean lifeguard for the Marine Safety Section of the Parks and Recreation Department of respondent, the City of Boca Raton, Florida (City). During this period, Faragher's immediate supervisors were Bill Terry, David Silverman, and Robert Gordon. In June 1990, Faragher resigned.

In 1992, Faragher brought an action against Terry, Silverman, and the City, asserting claims under Title VII, 42 U.S.C. § 1983, and Florida law. So far as it concerns the Title VII claim, the complaint alleged that Terry and Silverman created a "sexually hostile atmosphere" at the beach by repeatedly subjecting Faragher and other female lifeguards to "uninvited and offensive touching," by making lewd remarks, and by speaking of women in offensive terms. The complaint contained specific allegations that Terry once said that he would never promote a woman to the rank of lieutenant, and that Silverman had said to Faragher, "Date me or clean the toilets for a year." Asserting that Terry and Silverman were agents of the City, and that their conduct amounted to discrimination in the "terms, conditions, and privileges" of her employment. * * *

From time to time over the course of Faragher's tenure at the Marine Safety Section, between 4 and 6 of the 40 to 50 lifeguards were women. During that 5–year period, Terry repeatedly touched the bodies of female employees without invitation, would put his arm around Faragher, with his hand on her buttocks, and once made contact with another female lifeguard in a motion of sexual simulation. He made crudely demeaning references to women generally, and once commented disparagingly on Faragher's shape. During a job interview with a woman he hired as a lifeguard, Terry said that the female lifeguards had sex with their male counterparts and asked whether she would do the same.

Silverman behaved in similar ways. He once tackled Faragher and remarked that, but for a physical characteristic he found unattractive, he would readily have had sexual relations with her. Another time, he pantomimed an act of oral sex. Within earshot of the female lifeguards, Silverman made frequent, vulgar references to women and sexual matters, commented on the bodies of female lifeguards and beachgoers, and at least twice told female lifeguards that he would like to engage in sex with them.

Faragher did not complain to higher management about Terry or Silverman. * * *

In April 1990, however, two months before Faragher's resignation, Nancy Ewanchew, a former lifeguard, wrote to Richard Bender, the City's Personnel Director, complaining that Terry and Silverman had harassed her and other female lifeguards. Following investigation of this complaint, the City found that Terry and Silverman had behaved improperly, reprimanded them, and required them to choose between a suspension without pay or the forfeiture of annual leave.

* * * [The district court held in favor of Faragher but the Court of Appeals for the Eleventh Circuit reversed in an en banc opinion. It affirmed the ruling that the City did not have constructive knowledge of the harassment. It further held] that "an employer may be indirectly liable for hostile environment sexual harassment by a superior: (1) if the harassment occurs within the scope of the superior's employment; (2) if the employer assigns performance of a nondelegable duty to a supervisor and an employee is injured because of the supervisor's failure to carry out that duty; or (3) if there is an agency relationship which aids the supervisor's ability or opportunity to harass his subordinate."

Applying these principles, the court rejected Faragher's Title VII claim against the City. First, invoking standard agency language to classify the harassment by each supervisor as a "frolic" unrelated to his authorized tasks, the court found that in harassing Faragher, Terry and Silverman were acting outside of the scope of their employment and solely to further their own personal ends. Next, the court determined that the supervisors' agency relationship with the City did not assist them in perpetrating their harassment. Though noting that "a supervisor is always aided in accomplishing hostile environment sexual harassment by the existence of the agency relationship with his employer because his responsibilities include close proximity to and regular contact with the victim," the court held that traditional agency law does not employ so broad a concept of aid as a predicate of employer liability, but requires something more than a mere combination of agency relationship and improper conduct by the agent. * * *

Since our decision in Meritor, Courts of Appeals have struggled to derive manageable standards to govern employer liability for hostile environment harassment perpetrated by supervisory employees. While following our admonition to find guidance in the common law of agency, as embodied in the Restatement, the Courts of Appeals have adopted different approaches. [Citations.] We granted certiorari to address the divergence, and now reverse the judgment of the Eleventh Circuit and remand for entry of judgment in Faragher's favor.

* * * [I]n Harris [v. Forklift Systems, Inc., 510 U.S. 17, 114 S.Ct. 367, 126 L.Ed.2d 295 (1993)], we explained that in order to be actionable under the statute, a sexually objectionable environment must be both objectively and subjectively offensive, one that a reasonable person would find hostile or abusive, and one that the victim in fact did perceive to be so. We directed courts to determine whether an environment is sufficiently hostile or abusive by "looking at all the circumstances," including the "frequency of the discriminatory conduct; its severity; whether it is physically threatening or humiliating, or a mere offensive utterance; and whether it unreasonably interferes with an employee's work performance." Most recently, we explained that Title VII does not prohibit "genuine but innocuous differences in the ways men and women routinely interact with members of the same sex and of the opposite sex." Oncale v. Sundowner Offshore Services, Inc., 523 U.S. 75, ___, 118 S.Ct. 998, 1005, 140 L.Ed.2d 201 (1998). A recurring point in these opinions is that "simple teasing," offhand comments, and isolated incidents (unless extremely serious) will not amount to discriminatory changes in the "terms and conditions of employment."

These standards for judging hostility are sufficiently demanding to ensure that Title VII does not become a "general civility code." * * * We have made it clear that conduct must be extreme to amount to a change in the terms and conditions of employment, and the Courts of Appeals have heeded this view.

While indicating the substantive contours of the hostile environments forbidden by Title VII, our cases have established few definite rules for determining when an employer will be liable for a discriminatory environment that is otherwise actionably abusive. Given the circumstances of many of the litigated cases, including some that have come to us, it is not surprising that in many of them, the issue has been joined over the sufficiency of the abusive conditions, not the standards for determining an employer's liability for them. * * * Nor was it exceptional that standards for binding the employer were not in issue in Harris, supra. In that case of discrimination by hostile environment, the individual charged with creating the abusive atmosphere was the president of the corporate employer, who was indisputably within that class of an employer organization's officials who may be treated as the organization's proxy. * * *

Finally, there is nothing remarkable in the fact that claims against employers for discriminatory employment actions with tangible results, like hiring, firing, promotion, compensation, and work assignment, have resulted in employer liability once the discrimination was shown. See Meritor, 477 U.S., at 70–71, 106 S.Ct., at 2407–2408 (noting that "courts have consistently held employers liable for the discriminatory discharges of employees by supervisory personnel, whether or not the employer knew, should have known, or approved of the supervisor's actions"). * * *

A "master is subject to liability for the torts of his servants committed while acting in the scope of their employment." Restatement § 219(1). This doctrine has traditionally defined the "scope of employment" as including conduct "of the kind [a servant] is employed to perform," occurring "substantially within the authorized time and space limits," and "actuated, at least in part, by a purpose to serve the master," but as excluding an intentional use of force "unexpectable by the master." Id., § 228(1).

Courts of Appeals have typically held, or assumed, that conduct similar to the subject of this complaint falls outside the scope of employment. See, e.g., Harrison, 112 F.3d, at 1444 (sexual harassment " 'simply is not within the job description of any supervisor or any other worker in any reputable business' ") * * *. In so doing, the courts have emphasized that harassment consisting of unwelcome remarks and touching is motivated solely by individual desires and serves no purpose of the employer. For this reason, courts have likened hostile environment sexual harassment to the classic "frolic and detour" for which an employer has no vicarious liability. * * *

* * * [T]here is no reason to suppose that Congress wished courts to ignore the traditional distinction between acts falling within the scope and acts amounting to what the older law called frolics or detours from the course of employment. Such a distinction can readily be applied to the spectrum of possible harassing conduct by supervisors, as the following examples show. First, a supervisor might discriminate racially in job assignments in order to placate the prejudice pervasive in the labor force. Instances of this variety of the heckler's veto would be consciously intended to further the employer's interests by preserving peace in the workplace. Next, supervisors might reprimand male employees for workplace failings with banter, but respond to women's shortcomings in harsh or vulgar terms. A third example might be the supervisor who, as here, expresses his sexual interests in ways having no apparent object whatever of serving an interest of the employer. If a line is to be drawn between scope and frolic, it would lie between the first two examples and the third, and it thus makes sense in terms of traditional agency law to analyze the scope issue, in cases like the third example, just as most federal courts addressing that issue have done, classifying the harassment as beyond the scope of employment. * * *

The Court of Appeals also rejected vicarious liability on the part of the City insofar as it might rest on the concluding principle set forth in § 219(2)(d) of the Restatement, that an employer "is not subject to liability for the torts of his servants acting outside the scope of their employment unless ... the servant purported to act or speak on behalf of the principal and there was reliance on apparent authority, or he was aided in accomplishing the tort by the existence of the agency relation." Faragher points to several ways in which the agency relationship aided Terry and Silverman in carrying out their harassment. She argues that in general offending supervisors can abuse their authority to keep subordinates in their presence while they make offensive statements, and that they implicitly threaten to misuse their supervisory powers to deter any resistance or complaint. Thus, she maintains that power conferred on Terry and Silverman by the City enabled them to act for so long without provoking defiance or complaint.

The City, however, contends that § 219(2)(d) has no application here. It argues that the second qualification of the subsection, referring to a servant "aided in accomplishing the tort by the existence of the agency relation," merely "refines" the one preceding it, which holds the employer vicariously liable for its servant's abuse of apparent authority. Brief for Respondent 30–31, and n. 24. But this narrow reading is untenable; it would render the second qualification of § 219(2)(d) almost entirely superfluous (and would seem to ask us to shut our eyes to the potential effects of supervisory authority, even when not explicitly invoked). * * *

We therefore agree with Faragher that in implementing Title VII it makes sense to hold an employer vicariously liable for some tortious conduct of a supervisor made possible by abuse of his supervisory authority, and that the aided-by-agency-relation principle embodied in § 219(2)(d) of the Restatement provides an appropriate starting point for determining liability for the kind of harassment presented here.[3] * * * When a person with supervisory authority discriminates in the terms and conditions of subordinates' employment, his actions necessarily draw upon his superior position over the people who report to him, or those under them, whereas an employee generally cannot check a supervisor's abusive conduct the same way that she might deal with abuse from a co-worker. When a fellow employee harasses, the victim can walk away or tell the offender where to go, but it may be difficult to offer such responses to a supervisor, whose "power to supervise—[which may be] to hire and fire, and to set work schedules and pay rates—does not disappear ... when he chooses to harass through insults and offensive gestures rather than directly with threats of firing or promises of promotion." Estrich, Sex at Work, 43 Stan. L.Rev. 813, 854 (1991). Recognition of employer liability when discriminatory misuse of supervisory authority alters the terms and conditions of a victim's employment is underscored by the fact that the employer has a greater opportunity to guard against misconduct by supervisors than by common workers; employers have greater opportunity and incentive to screen them, train them, and monitor their performance.

In sum, there are good reasons for vicarious liability for misuse of supervisory authority. That rationale must, however, satisfy one more condition. We are not entitled to recognize this theory under Title VII unless we can square it with Meritor's holding that an employer is not "automatically" liable for harassment by a supervisor who creates the requisite degree of discrimination, and there is obviously some tension between that holding and the position that a supervisor's misconduct aided by supervisory authority subjects the employer to liability vicariously; if the "aid" may be the unspoken suggestion of retaliation by misuse of supervisory authority, the risk of automatic liability is high. To counter it, we think [the desirable approach is] to recognize an affirmative defense to liability in some circumstances, even when a supervisor has created the actionable environment.

[Under this approach, the employer is allowed] to show as an affirmative defense to liability that the employer had exercised reasonable care to avoid harassment and to eliminate it when it might occur, and that the complaining employee had failed to act with like reasonable care to take advantage of the employer's safeguards and otherwise to prevent harm that could have been avoided. This composite defense

---

3. We say "starting point" because our obligation here is not to make a pronouncement of agency law in general or to transplant § 219(2)(d) into Title VII. Rather, it is to adapt agency concepts to the practical objectives of Title VII. As we said in Meritor Savings Bank, FSB v. Vinson, 477 U.S. 57, 72, 106 S.Ct. 2399, 2408, 91 L.Ed.2d 49 (1986), "common-law principles may not be transferable in all their particulars to Title VII."

would, we think, implement the statute sensibly, for reasons that are not hard to fathom. * * *

In order to accommodate the principle of vicarious liability for harm caused by misuse of supervisory authority, as well as Title VII's equally basic policies of encouraging forethought by employers and saving action by objecting employees, we adopt the following holding in this case and in Burlington Industries, Inc. v. Ellerth, also decided today. An employer is subject to vicarious liability to a victimized employee for an actionable hostile environment created by a supervisor with immediate (or successively higher) authority over the employee. When no tangible employment action is taken, a defending employer may raise an affirmative defense to liability or damages, subject to proof by a preponderance of the evidence, see Fed. Rule. Civ. Proc. 8(c). The defense comprises two necessary elements: (a) that the employer exercised reasonable care to prevent and correct promptly any sexually harassing behavior, and (b) that the plaintiff employee unreasonably failed to take advantage of any preventive or corrective opportunities provided by the employer or to avoid harm otherwise. While proof that an employer had promulgated an antiharassment policy with complaint procedure is not necessary in every instance as a matter of law, the need for a stated policy suitable to the employment circumstances may appropriately be addressed in any case when litigating the first element of the defense. And while proof that an employee failed to fulfill the corresponding obligation of reasonable care to avoid harm is not limited to showing an unreasonable failure to use any complaint procedure provided by the employer, a demonstration of such failure will normally suffice to satisfy the employer's burden under the second element of the defense. No affirmative defense is available, however, when the supervisor's harassment culminates in a tangible employment action, such as discharge, demotion, or undesirable reassignment.

Applying these rules here, we believe that the judgment of the Court of Appeals must be reversed. The District Court found that the degree of hostility in the work environment rose to the actionable level and was attributable to Silverman and Terry. It is undisputed that these supervisors "were granted virtually unchecked authority" over their subordinates, "directly controll[ing] and supervis[ing] all aspects of [Faragher's] day-to-day activities." It is also clear that Faragher and her colleagues were "completely isolated from the City's higher management." The City did not seek review of these findings.

While the City would have an opportunity to raise an affirmative defense if there were any serious prospect of its presenting one, it appears from the record that any such avenue is closed. The District Court found that the City had entirely failed to disseminate its policy against sexual harassment among the beach employees and that its officials made no attempt to keep track of the conduct of supervisors like Terry and Silverman. The record also makes clear that the City's policy did not include any assurance that the harassing supervisors could be bypassed in registering complaints. Under such circumstances, we hold as a matter of law that the City could not be found to have exercised reasonable care to prevent the supervisors' harassing conduct. Unlike the employer of a small workforce, who might expect that sufficient care to prevent tortious behavior could be exercised informally, those responsible for city operations could not reasonably have thought that precautions against hostile environments in any one of many departments in far-flung locations could be effective without communicating some formal policy against harassment, with a sensible complaint procedure.

* * *

The judgment of the Court of Appeals for the Eleventh Circuit is reversed, and the case is remanded for reinstatement of the judgment of the District Court.

It is so ordered.

JUSTICE THOMAS, with whom JUSTICE SCALIA joins, dissenting.

For the reasons given in my dissenting opinion in Burlington Industries v. Ellerth, absent an adverse employment consequence, an employer cannot be held vicariously liable if a supervisor creates a hostile work environment. Petitioner suffered no adverse employment consequence; thus the Court of Appeals was correct to hold that the City is not vicariously liable for the conduct of Chief Terry and Lieutenant Silverman. Because the Court reverses this judgment, I dissent.

As for petitioner's negligence claim, the District Court made no finding as to the City's negligence, and the Court of Appeals did not directly consider the issue. I would therefore remand the case to the District Court for further proceedings on this question alone. I disagree with the Court's conclusion that merely because the City did not disseminate its sexual harassment policy, it should be liable as a matter of law. The City should be allowed to show either that: (1) there was a reasonably available avenue through which petitioner could have complained to a City official who supervised both Chief Terry and Lieutenant Silverman, or (2) it would not have learned of the harassment even if the policy had been distributed. * * *

Pagee 388: Remove *Goluszek* and insert:

ONCALE v. SUNDOWNER OFFSHORE SERVICES, INC.

Supreme Court of the United States, 1998.
523 U.S. 75, 118 S.Ct. 998, 140 L.Ed.2d 201.

JUSTICE SCALIA delivered the opinion of the Court.

This case presents the question whether workplace harassment can violate Title VII's prohibition against "discriminat[ion] ... because of ... sex," 42 U.S.C. § 2000e-2(a)(1), when the harasser and the harassed employee are of the same sex. *ISSUE*

The District Court having granted summary judgment for respondent, we must assume the facts to be as alleged by petitioner Joseph

— DIST. CT. → SUMMARY JUDGMENT FOR RESPONDENT

Oncale. The precise details are irrelevant to the legal point we must decide, and in the interest of both brevity and dignity we shall describe them only generally. In late October 1991, Oncale was working for respondent Sundowner Offshore Services on a Chevron U.S. A., Inc., oil platform in the Gulf of Mexico. He was employed as a roustabout on an eight-man crew which included respondents John Lyons, Danny Pippen, and Brandon Johnson. Lyons, the crane operator, and Pippen, the driller, had supervisory authority. On several occasions, Oncale was forcibly subjected to sex-related, humiliating actions against him by Lyons, Pippen and Johnson in the presence of the rest of the crew. Pippen and Lyons also physically assaulted Oncale in a sexual manner, and Lyons threatened him with rape.

Oncale's complaints to supervisory personnel produced no remedial action; in fact, the company's Safety Compliance Clerk, Valent Hohen, told Oncale that Lyons and Pippen "picked [on] him all the time too," and called him a name suggesting homosexuality. Oncale eventually quit—asking that his pink slip reflect that he "voluntarily left due to sexual harassment and verbal abuse." When asked at his deposition why he left Sundowner, Oncale stated "I felt that if I didn't leave my job, that I would be raped or forced to have sex."

Oncale filed a complaint against Sundowner in the United States District Court for the Eastern District of Louisiana, alleging that he was discriminated against in his employment because of his sex. Relying on the Fifth Circuit's decision in Garcia v. Elf Atochem North America, 28 F.3d 446, 451–452 (C.A.5 1994), the district court held that "Mr. Oncale, a male, has no cause of action under Title VII for harassment by male co-workers." On appeal, a panel of the Fifth Circuit concluded that Garcia was binding Circuit precedent, and affirmed. 83 F.3d 118 (1996). We granted certiorari.

* * *

Title VII's prohibition of discrimination "because of ... sex" protects men as well as women, [citation], and in the related context of racial discrimination in the workplace we have rejected any conclusive presumption that an employer will not discriminate against members of his own race. [Citation.] In Johnson v. Transportation Agency, Santa Clara City., 480 U.S. 616, 107 S.Ct. 1442, 94 L.Ed.2d 615 (1987), a male employee claimed that his employer discriminated against him because of his sex when it preferred a female employee for promotion. Although we ultimately rejected the claim on other grounds, we did not consider it significant that the supervisor who made that decision was also a man. If our precedents leave any doubt on the question, we hold today that nothing in Title VII necessarily bars a claim of discrimination "because of ... sex" merely because the plaintiff and the defendant (or the person charged with acting on behalf of the defendant) are of the same sex.

Courts have had little trouble with that principle in cases like Johnson, where an employee claims to have been passed over for a job or promotion. But when the issue arises in the context of a "hostile environment" sexual harassment claim, the state and federal courts have taken a bewildering variety of stances. Some, like the Fifth Circuit in this case, have held that same-sex sexual harassment claims are never cognizable under Title VII. See also, e.g., Goluszek v. H.P. Smith, 697 F.Supp. 1452 (N.D.Ill.1988). Other decisions say that such claims are actionable only if the plaintiff can prove that the harasser is homosexual (and thus presumably motivated by sexual desire). Compare McWilliams v. Fairfax County Board of Supervisors, 72 F.3d 1191 (C.A.4 1996), with Wrightson v. Pizza Hut of America, 99 F.3d 138 (C.A.4 1996). Still others suggest that workplace harassment that is sexual in content is always actionable, regardless of the harasser's sex, sexual orientation, or motivations. See Doe v. Belleville, 119 F.3d 563 (C.A.7 1997).

[margin note: FED CTS. SPLIT ON WHETHER "HOSTILE ENVIRON" SEX HARASSMENT CLAIMS ALLOWED FOR SAME-SEX π & Δ]

We see no justification in the statutory language or our precedents for a categorical rule excluding same-sex harassment claims from the coverage of Title VII. As some courts have observed, male-on-male sexual harassment in the workplace was assuredly not the principal evil Congress was concerned with when it enacted Title VII. But statutory prohibitions often go beyond the principal evil to cover reasonably comparable evils, and it is ultimately the provisions of our laws rather than the principal concerns of our legislators by which we are governed. Title VII prohibits "discriminat[ion] . . . because of . . . sex" in the "terms" or "conditions" of employment. Our holding that this includes sexual harassment must extend to sexual harassment of any kind that meets the statutory requirements.

Respondents and their amici contend that recognizing liability for same-sex harassment will transform Title VII into a general civility code for the American workplace. But that risk is no greater for same-sex than for opposite-sex harassment, and is adequately met by careful attention to the requirements of the statute. Title VII does not prohibit all verbal or physical harassment in the workplace; it is directed only at "discriminat[ion] . . . because of . . . sex." We have never held that workplace harassment, even harassment between men and women, is automatically discrimination because of sex merely because the words used have sexual content or connotations. "The critical issue, Title VII's text indicates, is whether members of one sex are exposed to disadvantageous terms or conditions of employment to which members of the other sex are not exposed." Harris, supra, at 25, 114 S.Ct., at 372 (GINSBURG, J., concurring).

[margin note: RESPONDENT's CLAIM]

Courts and juries have found the inference of discrimination easy to draw in most male-female sexual harassment situations, because the challenged conduct typically involves explicit or implicit proposals of sexual activity; it is reasonable to assume those proposals would not have been made to someone of the same sex. The same chain of inference would be available to a plaintiff alleging same-sex harassment, if there were credible evidence that the harasser was homosexual. But harassing conduct need not be motivated by sexual desire to support an inference of discrimination on the basis of sex. A trier of fact might reasonably find such discrimination, for example, if a female victim is harassed in

[margin note: SAME-SEX HARASSMENT NEED NOT BE MOTIVATED BY SEXUAL DESIRE TO SUPPORT INFERENCE OF DISCRIMINATION ON BASIS OF SEX]

such sex-specific and derogatory terms by another woman as to make it clear that the harasser is motivated by general hostility to the presence of women in the workplace. A same-sex harassment plaintiff may also, of course, offer direct comparative evidence about how the alleged harasser treated members of both sexes in a mixed-sex workplace. Whatever evidentiary route the plaintiff chooses to follow, he or she must always prove that the conduct at issue was not merely tinged with offensive sexual connotations, but actually constituted "discrimina[tion] . . . because of . . . sex."

And there is another requirement that prevents Title VII from expanding into a general civility code: As we emphasized in Meritor and Harris, the statute does not reach genuine but innocuous differences in the ways men and women routinely interact with members of the same sex and of the opposite sex. The prohibition of harassment on the basis of sex requires neither asexuality nor androgyny in the workplace; it forbids only behavior so objectively offensive as to alter the "conditions" of the victim's employment. "Conduct that is not severe or pervasive enough to create an objectively hostile or abusive work environment—an environment that a reasonable person would find hostile or abusive—is beyond Title VII's purview." [Citation.] We have always regarded that requirement as crucial, and as sufficient to ensure that courts and juries do not mistake ordinary socializing in the workplace—such as male-on-male horseplay or intersexual flirtation—for discriminatory "conditions of employment."

We have emphasized, moreover, that the objective severity of harassment should be judged from the perspective of a reasonable person in the plaintiff's position, considering "all the circumstances." [Citation.] In same-sex (as in all) harassment cases, that inquiry requires careful consideration of the social context in which particular behavior occurs and is experienced by its target. A professional football player's working environment is not severely or pervasively abusive, for example, if the coach smacks him on the buttocks as he heads onto the field—even if the same behavior would reasonably be experienced as abusive by the coach's secretary (male or female) back at the office. The real social impact of workplace behavior often depends on a constellation of surrounding circumstances, expectations, and relationships which are not fully captured by a simple recitation of the words used or the physical acts performed. Common sense, and an appropriate sensitivity to social context, will enable courts and juries to distinguish between simple teasing or roughhousing among members of the same sex, and conduct which a reasonable person in the plaintiff's position would find severely hostile or abusive.

Because we conclude that sex discrimination consisting of same-sex sexual harassment is actionable under Title VII, the judgment of the Court of Appeals for the Fifth Circuit is reversed, and the case is remanded for further proceedings consistent with this opinion.

It is so ordered.

Part V

DEFINING PROTECTED CLASSES

Chapter 16

SEXUAL ORIENTATION

Page 534: Sexual Orientation

As noted in the text numerous states have enacted statutes and local governments ordinances that proscribe discrimination on the basis of sexual orientation. A political reaction has been to amend constitutions through popular initiatives, or otherwise, that restrict enactments of such legislation. The Supreme Court addressed the constitutionality of one such initiative in **ROMER v. EVANS**, 517 U.S. 620, 116 S.Ct. 1620, 134 L.Ed.2d 855 (1996). In this case the Court held unconstitutional a Colorado constitutional amendment, known as Amendment 2, which was submitted to a public referendum and adopted. It read:

"No Protected Status Based on Homosexual, Lesbian, or Bisexual Orientation. Neither the State of Colorado, through any of its branches or departments, nor any of its agencies, political subdivisions, municipalities or school districts, shall enact, adopt or enforce any statute, regulation, ordinance or policy whereby homosexual, lesbian or bisexual orientation, conduct, practices or relationships shall constitute or otherwise be the basis of or entitle any person or class of persons to have or claim any minority status, quota preferences, protected status or claim of discrimination. This Section of the Constitution shall be in all respects self-executing."

The state argued that this amendment did not violate the Equal Protection Clause of the Fourteenth Amendment of the federal Constitution because it put gays and lesbians in the same position as all other persons and therefore that the measure did no more than deny homosexuals special rights. The Court rejected this reasoning and noted that this reading of the amendment was "implausible." Writing for the majority, Justice Kennedy explained:

"Sweeping and comprehensive is the change in legal status effected by this law. So much is evident from the ordinances that the Colorado Supreme Court declared would be void by operation of Amendment 2. Homosexuals, by state decree, are put in a solitary class with respect to transactions and relations in both the private and governmental spheres. The amendment withdraws from homosexuals, but no others, specific legal protection from the injuries caused by discrimination, and it forbids reinstatement of these laws and policies. * * *

"The Fourteenth Amendment's promise that no person shall be denied the equal protection of the laws must co-exist with the practical necessity that most legislation classifies for one purpose or another, with resulting disadvantage to various groups or persons. We have attempted to reconcile the principle with the reality by stating that, if a law neither burdens a fundamental right nor targets a suspect class, we will uphold the legislative classification so long as it bears a rational relation to some legitimate end.

"Amendment 2 fails, indeed defies, even this conventional inquiry. First, the amendment has the peculiar property of imposing a broad and undifferentiated disability on a single named group, an exceptional and, as we shall explain, invalid form of legislation. Second, its sheer breadth is so discontinuous with the reasons offered for it that the amendment seems inexplicable by anything but animus toward the class that it affects; it lacks a rational relationship to legitimate state interests. * * *

"A second and related point is that laws of the kind now before us raise the inevitable inference that the disadvantage imposed is born of animosity toward the class of persons affected. '[I]f the constitutional conception of "equal protection of the laws" means anything, it must at the very least mean that a bare ... desire to harm a politically unpopular group cannot constitute a legitimate governmental interest.' Even laws enacted for broad and ambitious purposes often can be explained by reference to legitimate public policies which justify the incidental disadvantages they impose on certain persons. Amendment 2, however, in making a general announcement that gays and lesbians shall not have any particular protections from the law, inflicts on them immediate, continuing, and real injuries that outrun and belie any legitimate justifications that may be claimed for it. We conclude that, in addition to the far-reaching deficiencies of Amendment 2 that we have noted, the principles it offends, in another sense, are conventional and venerable; a law must bear a rational relationship to a legitimate governmental purpose, and Amendment 2 does not. * * *

"We must conclude that Amendment 2 classifies homosexuals not to further a proper legislative end but to make them unequal to everyone else. This Colorado cannot do. A State cannot so deem a class of persons a stranger to its laws. Amendment 2 violates the Equal Protection Clause, and the judgment of the Supreme Court of Colorado is affirmed."

Justice Scalia wrote a dissenting opinion that was joined by Chief Justice Rehnquist and Justice Thomas. It noted:

"The Court has mistaken a Kulturkampf for a fit of spite. The constitutional amendment before us here is not the manifestation of a ' "bare ... desire to harm" ' homosexuals, but is rather a modest attempt by seemingly tolerant Coloradans to preserve traditional sexual mores against the efforts of a politically powerful minority to revise those mores through use of the laws. That objective, and the means chosen to achieve it, are not only unimpeachable under any constitutional doctrine hitherto pronounced (hence the opinion's heavy reliance upon principles of righteousness rather than judicial holdings); they have been specifi-

cally approved by the Congress of the United States and by this Court.
* * *

"The Court's opinion contains grim, disapproving hints that Coloradans have been guilty of 'animus' or 'animosity' toward homosexuality, as though that has been established as Unamerican. Of course it is our moral heritage that one should not hate any human being or class of human beings. But I had thought that one could consider certain conduct reprehensible—murder, for example, or polygamy, or cruelty to animals—and could exhibit even 'animus' toward such conduct. Surely that is the only sort of 'animus' at issue here: moral disapproval of homosexual conduct, the same sort of moral disapproval that produced the centuries-old criminal laws that we held constitutional in Bowers."
* * *

Chapter 18

DISCRIMINATION ON THE
BASIS OF DISABILITY

C. CONCEPTS OF DISABILITY
DISCRIMINATION

1. DEFINING "DISABILITY"

Page 579: Discrimination on the Basis of Disability

In 1998 and 1999 the Supreme Court delivered a number of major decisions concerning the definition of "disability."

BRAGDON v. ABBOTT

Supreme Court of the United States, 1998.
524 U.S. 624, 118 S.Ct. 21968, 141 L.Ed.2d 540.

JUSTICE KENNEDY delivered the opinion of the Court.

We address in this case the application of the Americans with Disabilities Act of 1990 (ADA) to persons infected with the human immunodeficiency virus (HIV). We granted certiorari to review, first, whether HIV infection is a disability under the ADA when the infection has not yet progressed to the so-called symptomatic phase; and, second, whether the Court of Appeals, in affirming a grant of summary judgment, cited sufficient material in the record to determine, as a matter of law, that respondent's infection with HIV posed no direct threat to the health and safety of her treating dentist.

I

Respondent Sidney Abbott has been infected with HIV since 1986. When the incidents we recite occurred, her infection had not manifested its most serious symptoms. On September 16, 1994, she went to the office of petitioner Randon Bragdon in Bangor, Maine, for a dental appointment. She disclosed her HIV infection on the patient registration form. Petitioner completed a dental examination, discovered a cavity, and informed respondent of his policy against filling cavities of HIV-infected patients. He offered to perform the work at a hospital with no added fee for his services, though respondent would be responsible for the cost of using the hospital's facilities. Respondent declined.

Respondent sued petitioner under state law and § 302 of the ADA, alleging discrimination on the basis of her disability. The state law claims are not before us. Section 302 of the ADA provides:

> "No individual shall be discriminated against on the basis of disability in the full and equal enjoyment of the goods, services, facilities, privileges, advantages, or accommodations of any place of public accommodation by any person who ... operates a place of public accommodation." § 12182(a). [Note: The employment discrimination section of the ADA, 42 U.S.C.A. 12112, has distinct but similar language: "No covered entity shall discriminate against a qualified individual in regard to job application procedures, the hiring, advancement, or discharge of employees, employee compensation, job training, and other terms, conditions, and privileges of employment." Ed.]

The term "public accommodation" is defined to include the "professional office of a health care provider." § 12181(7)(F).

A later subsection qualifies the mandate not to discriminate. It provides:

> "Nothing in this subchapter shall require an entity to permit an individual to participate in or benefit from the goods, services, facilities, privileges, advantages and accommodations of such entity where such individual poses a direct threat to the health or safety of others." § 12182(b)(3). [Note: the employment discrimination section of the ADA, 42 U.S.C.A. 12113(b) has a similar provision: "The term 'qualification standards' may include a requirement that an individual shall not pose a direct threat to the health or safety of other individuals in the workplace." Ed.]

* * *

The District Court ruled in favor of the plaintiffs, holding that respondent's HIV infection satisfied the ADA's definition of disability. The court held further that petitioner raised no genuine issue of material fact as to whether respondent's HIV infection would have posed a direct threat to the health or safety of others during the course of a dental treatment.

The Court of Appeals affirmed. * * *

II

WHETHER RESPONDENT'S DISABILITY HIV INFECTION A DISABILITY UNDER ADA

We first review the ruling that respondent's HIV infection constituted a disability under the ADA. The statute defines disability as:

> "(A) a physical or mental impairment that substantially limits one or more of the major life activities of such individual;
>
> "(B) a record of such an impairment; or
>
> "(C) being regarded as having such impairment." § 12102(2).

We hold respondent's HIV infection was a disability under subsection (A) of the definitional section of the statute. In light of this conclusion, we need not consider the applicability of subsections (B) or (C).

Our consideration of subsection (A) of the definition proceeds in three steps. First, we consider whether respondent's HIV infection was a physical impairment. Second, we identify the life activity upon which respondent relies (reproduction and child bearing) and determine whether it constitutes a major life activity under the ADA. Third, tying the two statutory phrases together, we ask whether the impairment substantially limited the major life activity. In construing the statute, we are informed by interpretations of parallel definitions in previous statutes and the views of various administrative agencies which have faced this interpretive question.

A

The ADA's definition of disability is drawn almost verbatim from the definition of "handicapped individual" included in the Rehabilitation Act of 1973 and the definition of "handicap" contained in the Fair Housing Amendments Act of 1988. Congress' repetition of a well-established term carries the implication that Congress intended the term to be construed in accordance with pre-existing regulatory interpretations. In this case, Congress did more than suggest this construction; it adopted a specific statutory provision in the ADA directing as follows:

> "Except as otherwise provided in this chapter, nothing in this chapter shall be construed to apply a lesser standard than the standards applied under title V of the Rehabilitation Act of 1973 or the regulations issued by Federal agencies pursuant to such title." 42 U.S.C. § 12201(a).

The directive requires us to construe the ADA to grant at least as much protection as provided by the regulations implementing the Rehabilitation Act.

1

The first step in the inquiry under subsection (A) requires us to determine whether respondent's condition constituted a physical impairment. The Department of Health, Education and Welfare (HEW) issued the first regulations interpreting the Rehabilitation Act in 1977. The regulations are of particular significance because, at the time, HEW was the agency responsible for coordinating the implementation and enforcement of § 504. The HEW regulations, which appear without change in the current regulations issued by the Department of Health and Human Services, define "physical or mental impairment" to mean:

> "(A) any physiological disorder or condition, cosmetic disfigurement, or anatomical loss affecting one or more of the following body systems: neurological; musculoskeletal; special sense organs; respiratory, including speech organs; cardiovascular; reproductive, digestive, genito-urinary; hemic and lymphatic; skin; and endocrine; or

"(B) any mental or psychological disorder, such as mental retardation, organic brain syndrome, emotional or mental illness, and specific learning disabilities." 45 CFR § 84.3(j)(2)(i) (1997).

In issuing these regulations, HEW decided against including a list of disorders constituting physical or mental impairments, out of concern that any specific enumeration might not be comprehensive. 45 CFR pt. 84, App. A, p. 334 (1997). The commentary accompanying the regulations, however, contains a representative list of disorders and conditions constituting physical impairments, including "such diseases and conditions as orthopedic, visual, speech, and hearing impairments, cerebral palsy, epilepsy, muscular dystrophy, multiple sclerosis, cancer, heart disease, diabetes, mental retardation, emotional illness, and ... drug addiction and alcoholism."

In 1980, the President transferred responsibility for the implementation and enforcement of § 504 to the Attorney General. The regulations issued by the Justice Department, which remain in force to this day, adopted verbatim the HEW definition of physical impairment quoted above. 28 CFR § 41.31(b)(1) (1997). In addition, the representative list of diseases and conditions originally relegated to the commentary accompanying the HEW regulations were incorporated into the text of the regulations.

HIV infection is not included in the list of specific disorders constituting physical impairments, in part because HIV was not identified as the cause of AIDS until 1983. HIV infection does fall well within the general definition set forth by the regulations, however.

The disease follows a predictable and, as of today, an unalterable course. Once a person is infected with HIV, the virus invades different cells in the blood and in body tissues. * * *

The initial stage of HIV infection is known as acute or primary HIV infection. In a typical case, this stage lasts three months. The virus concentrates in the blood. The assault on the immune system is immediate. The victim suffers from a sudden and serious decline in the number of white blood cells. There is no latency period. Mononucleosis-like symptoms often emerge between six days and six weeks after infection, at times accompanied by fever, headache, enlargement of the lymph nodes (lymphadenopathy), muscle pain (myalgia), rash, lethargy, gastrointestinal disorders, and neurological disorders. Usually these symptoms abate within 14 to 21 days. HIV antibodies appear in the bloodstream within 3 weeks; circulating HIV can be detected within 10 weeks.

After the symptoms associated with the initial stage subside, the disease enters what is referred to sometimes as its asymptomatic phase. The term is a misnomer, in some respects, for clinical features persist throughout, including lymphadenopathy, dermatological disorders, oral lesions, and bacterial infections. Although it varies with each individual, in most instances this stage lasts from 7 to 11 years. The virus now tends to concentrate in the lymph nodes, though low levels of the virus continue to appear in the blood. It was once thought the virus became inactive during this period, but it is now known that the relative lack of symptoms is attributable to the virus' migration from the circulatory system into the lymph nodes. The migration reduces the viral presence in other parts of the body, with a corresponding diminution in physical manifestations of the disease. The virus, however, thrives in the lymph nodes, which, as a vital point of the body's immune response system, represents an ideal environment for the infection of other CD4+ cells. Studies have shown that viral production continues at a high rate. CD4+ cells continue to decline an average of 5% to 10% (40 to 80 cells/mm3) per year throughout this phase.

A person is regarded as having AIDS when his or her CD4+ count drops below 200 cells/mm3 of blood or when CD4+ cells comprise less than 14% of his or her total lymphocytes. During this stage, the clinical conditions most often associated with HIV, such as pneumocystis carinii pneumonia, Kaposi's sarcoma, and non-Hodgkins lymphoma, tend to appear. In addition, the general systemic disorders present during all stages of the disease, such as fever, weight loss, fatigue, lesions, nausea, and diarrhea, tend to worsen. In most cases, once the patient's CD4+ count drops below 10 cells/mm3, death soon follows.

In light of the immediacy with which the virus begins to damage the infected person's white blood cells and the severity of the disease, we hold it is an impairment from the moment of infection. As noted earlier, infection with HIV causes immediate abnormalities in a person's blood, and the infected person's white cell count continues to drop throughout the course of the disease, even when the attack is concentrated in the lymph nodes. In light of these facts, HIV infection must be regarded as a physiological disorder with a constant and detrimental effect on the infected person's hemic and lymphatic systems from the moment of infection. HIV infection satisfies the statutory and regulatory definition of a physical impairment during every stage of the disease.

2

The statute is not operative, and the definition not satisfied, unless the impairment affects a major life activity. Respondent's claim throughout this case has been that the HIV infection placed a substantial limitation on her ability to reproduce and to bear children. Given the pervasive, and invariably fatal, course of the disease, its effect on major life activities of many sorts might have been relevant to our inquiry. Respondent and a number of amici make arguments about HIV's profound impact on almost every phase of the infected person's life. In light of these submissions, it may seem legalistic to circumscribe our discussion to the activity of reproduction. We have little doubt that had different parties brought the suit they would have maintained that an HIV infection imposes substantial limitations on other major life activities.

From the outset, however, the case has been treated as one in which reproduction was the major life activity limited by the impairment. It is our practice to decide cases on the grounds raised and considered in the

REPRODUCTION
↓
MAJOR LIFE
ACTIVITY ?

Court of Appeals and included in the question on which we granted certiorari. We ask, then, whether reproduction is a major life activity.

We have little difficulty concluding that it is. As the Court of Appeals held, "[t]he plain meaning of the word 'major' denotes comparative importance" and "suggest[s] that the touchstone for determining an activity's inclusion under the statutory rubric is its significance." Reproduction falls well within the phrase "major life activity." Reproduction and the sexual dynamics surrounding it are central to the life process itself.

While petitioner concedes the importance of reproduction, he claims that Congress intended the ADA only to cover those aspects of a person's life which have a public, economic, or daily character. The argument founders on the statutory language. Nothing in the definition suggests that activities without a public, economic, or daily dimension may somehow be regarded as so unimportant or insignificant as to fall outside the meaning of the word "major." The breadth of the term confounds the attempt to limit its construction in this manner.

As we have noted, the ADA must be construed to be consistent with regulations issued to implement the Rehabilitation Act. Rather than enunciating a general principle for determining what is and is not a major life activity, the Rehabilitation Act regulations instead provide a representative list, defining term to include "functions such as caring for one's self, performing manual tasks, walking, seeing, hearing, speaking, breathing, learning, and working." As the use of the term "such as" confirms, the list is illustrative, not exhaustive.

These regulations are contrary to petitioner's attempt to limit the meaning of the term "major" to public activities. The inclusion of activities such as caring for one's self and performing manual tasks belies the suggestion that a task must have a public or economic character in order to be a major life activity for purposes of the ADA. On the contrary, the Rehabilitation Act regulations support the inclusion of reproduction as a major life activity, since reproduction could not be regarded as any less important than working and learning. Petitioner advances no credible basis for confining major life activities to those with a public, economic, or daily aspect. In the absence of any reason to reach a contrary conclusion, we agree with the Court of Appeals' determination that reproduction is a major life activity for the purposes of the ADA.

3

The final element of the disability definition in subsection (A) is whether respondent's physical impairment was a substantial limit on the major life activity she asserts. The Rehabilitation Act regulations provide no additional guidance.

Our evaluation of the medical evidence leads us to conclude that respondent's infection substantially limited her ability to reproduce in two independent ways. First, a woman infected with HIV who tries to conceive a child imposes on the man a significant risk of becoming infected. The cumulative results of 13 studies collected in a 1994 textbook on AIDS indicates that 20% of male partners of women with HIV became HIV-positive themselves, with a majority of the studies finding a statistically significant risk of infection.

Second, an infected woman risks infecting her child during gestation and childbirth, i.e., perinatal transmission. Petitioner concedes that women infected with HIV face about a 25% risk of transmitting the virus to their children. * * *

The Act addresses substantial limitations on major life activities, not utter inabilities. Conception and childbirth are not impossible for an HIV victim but, without doubt, are dangerous to the public health. This meets the definition of a substantial limitation. The decision to reproduce carries economic and legal consequences as well. There are added costs for antiretroviral therapy, supplemental insurance, and long-term health care for the child who must be examined and, tragic to think, treated for the infection. The laws of some States, moreover, forbid persons infected with HIV from having sex with others, regardless of consent.

In the end, the disability definition does not turn on personal choice. When significant limitations result from the impairment, the definition is met even if the difficulties are not insurmountable. For the statistical and other reasons we have cited, of course, the limitations on reproduction may be insurmountable here. Testimony from the respondent that her HIV infection controlled her decision not to have a child is unchallenged. We agree with the District Court and the Court of Appeals that no triable issue of fact impedes a ruling on the question of statutory coverage. Respondent's HIV infection is a physical impairment which substantially limits a major life activity, as the ADA defines it. In view of our holding, we need not address the second question presented, i.e., whether HIV infection is a per se disability under the ADA.

B

Our holding is confirmed by a consistent course of agency interpretation before and after enactment of the ADA. Every agency to consider the issue under the Rehabilitation Act found statutory coverage for persons with asymptomatic HIV. * * * It is enough to observe that the well-reasoned views of the agencies implementing a statute "constitute a body of experience and informed judgment to which courts and litigants may properly resort for guidance."

One comprehensive and significant administrative precedent is a 1988 opinion issued by the Office of Legal Counsel of the Department of Justice (OLC) concluding that the Rehabilitation Act "protects symptomatic and asymptomatic HIV-infected individuals against discrimination in any covered program." * * * OLC determined further that asymptomatic HIV imposed a substantial limit on the major life activity of reproduction. The Opinion said:

"Based on the medical knowledge available to us, we believe that it is reasonable to conclude that the life activity of procreation ... is substantially limited for an asymptomatic HIV-infected individual. In light of the significant risk that the AIDS virus may be transmitted to a baby during pregnancy, HIV-infected individuals cannot, whether they are male or female, engage in the act of procreation with the normal expectation of bringing forth a healthy child."

In addition, OLC indicated that "[t]he life activity of engaging in sexual relations is threatened and probably substantially limited by the contagiousness of the virus." Either consideration was sufficient to render asymptomatic HIV infection a handicap for purposes of the Rehabilitation Act. * * *

Every court which addressed the issue before the ADA was enacted in July 1990, moreover, concluded that asymptomatic HIV infection satisfied the Rehabilitation Act's definition of a handicap.* * *

Had Congress done nothing more than copy the Rehabilitation Act definition into the ADA, its action would indicate the new statute should be construed in light of this unwavering line of administrative and judicial interpretation. All indications are that Congress was well aware of the position taken by OLC when enacting the ADA and intended to give that position its active endorsement. * * *

We find the uniformity of the administrative and judicial precedent construing the definition significant. When administrative and judicial interpretations have settled the meaning of an existing statutory provision, repetition of the same language in a new statute indicates, as a general matter, the intent to incorporate its administrative and judicial interpretations as well. The uniform body of administrative and judicial precedent confirms the conclusion we reach today as the most faithful way to effect the congressional design.

C

* * *

We also draw guidance from the views of the agencies authorized to administer other sections of the ADA. Most categorical of all is EEOC's conclusion that "an individual who has HIV infection (including asymptomatic HIV infection) is an individual with a disability." EEOC Interpretive Manual § 902.4(c)(1), p. 902–21; In the EEOC's view, "impairments ... such as HIV infection, are inherently substantially limiting." 29 CFR pt. 1630, App., p. 350 (1997).

The regulatory authorities we cite are consistent with our holding that HIV infection, even in the so-called asymptomatic phase, is an impairment which substantially limits the major life activity of reproduction.

III

* * *

Notwithstanding the protection given respondent by the ADA's definition of disability, petitioner could have refused to treat her if her infectious condition "pose[d] a direct threat to the health or safety of others." The ADA defines a direct threat to be "a significant risk to the health or safety of others that cannot be eliminated by a modification of policies, practices, or procedures or by the provision of auxiliary aids or services." Parallel provisions appear in the employment provisions of Title I.

The ADA's direct threat provision stems from the recognition in School Bd. of Nassau Cty. v. Arline, 480 U.S. 273, 287, 107 S.Ct. 1123, 1130–1131, 94 L.Ed.2d 307 (1987), of the importance of prohibiting discrimination against individuals with disabilities while protecting others from significant health and safety risks, resulting, for instance, from a contagious disease. In Arline, the Court reconciled these objectives by construing the Rehabilitation Act not to require the hiring of a person who posed "a significant risk of communicating an infectious disease to others." Congress amended the Rehabilitation Act and the Fair Housing Act to incorporate the language. It later relied on the same language in enacting the ADA. Because few, if any, activities in life are risk free, Arline and the ADA do not ask whether a risk exists, but whether it is significant.

The existence, or nonexistence, of a significant risk must be determined from the standpoint of the person who refuses the treatment or accommodation, and the risk assessment must be based on medical or other objective evidence. As a health care professional, petitioner had the duty to assess the risk of infection based on the objective, scientific information available to him and others in his profession. His belief that a significant risk existed, even if maintained in good faith, would not relieve him from liability. To use the words of the question presented, petitioner receives no special deference simply because he is a health care professional. It is true that Arline reserved "the question whether courts should also defer to the reasonable medical judgments of private physicians on which an employer has relied." At most, this statement reserved the possibility that employers could consult with individual physicians as objective third-party experts. It did not suggest that an individual physician's state of mind could excuse discrimination without regard to the objective reasonableness of his actions.

Our conclusion that courts should assess the objective reasonableness of the views of health care professionals without deferring to their individual judgments does not answer the implicit assumption in the question presented, whether petitioner's actions were reasonable in light of the available medical evidence. In assessing the reasonableness of petitioner's actions, the views of public health authorities, such as the U.S. Public Health Service, CDC, and the National Institutes of Health, are of special weight and authority. The views of these organizations are not conclusive, however. A health care professional who disagrees with the prevailing medical consensus may refute it by citing a credible scientific basis for deviating from the accepted norm.

We have reviewed so much of the record as necessary to illustrate the application of the rule to the facts of this case. For the most part, the Court of Appeals followed the proper standard in evaluating the petitioner's position and conducted a thorough review of the evidence.* * * Petitioner failed to present any objective, medical evidence showing that treating respondent in a hospital would be safer or more efficient in preventing HIV transmission than treatment in a well-equipped dental office.

We are concerned, however, that the Court of Appeals might have placed mistaken reliance upon two other sources. In ruling no triable issue of fact existed on this point, the Court of Appeals relied on the 1993 CDC Dentistry Guidelines and the 1991 American Dental Association Policy on HIV. This evidence is not definitive.* * *

We conclude the proper course is to give the Court of Appeals the opportunity to determine whether our analysis of some of the studies cited by the parties would change its conclusion that petitioner presented neither objective evidence nor a triable issue of fact on the question of risk. In remanding the case, we do not foreclose the possibility that the Court of Appeals may reach the same conclusion it did earlier. A remand will permit a full exploration of the issue through the adversary process.

The determination of the Court of Appeals that respondent's HIV infection was a disability under the ADA is affirmed. The judgment is vacated, and the case is remanded for further proceedings consistent with this opinion.

It is so ordered.

Justice Stevens, with whom Justice Breyer joins, concurring.

The Court's opinion demonstrates that respondent's HIV infection easily falls within the statute's definition of "disability." Moreover, the Court's discussion in Part III of the relevant evidence has persuaded me that the judgment of the Court of Appeals should be affirmed. I do not believe petitioner has sustained his burden of adducing evidence sufficient to raise a triable issue of fact on the significance of the risk posed by treating respondent in his office. * * * Because I am in agreement with the legal analysis in Justice KENNEDY's opinion, in order to provide a judgment supported by a majority, I join that opinion even though I would prefer an outright affirmance.

Justice Ginsburg, concurring.

HIV infection, as the description set out in the Court's opinion documents has been regarded as a disease limiting life itself. The disease inevitably pervades life's choices: education, employment, family and financial undertakings. It affects the need for and, as this case shows, the ability to obtain health care because of the reaction of others to the impairment. No rational legislator, it seems to me apparent, would require nondiscrimination once symptoms become visible but permit discrimination when the disease, though present, is not yet visible. I am therefore satisfied that the statutory and regulatory definitions are well met. HIV infection is "a physical ... impairment that substantially limits ... major life activities," or is so perceived, including the afflicted individual's family relations, employment potential, and ability to care for herself.

I further agree, in view of the "importance [of the issue] to health care workers," that it is wise to remand, erring, if at all, on the side of caution. By taking this course, the Court ensures a fully informed determination whether respondent Abbott's disease posed "a significant risk to the health or safety of [petitioner Bragdon] that [could not] be eliminated by a modification of policies, practices, or procedures...."

CHIEF JUSTICE REHNQUIST, with whom JUSTICE SCALIA and JUSTICE THOMAS join, and with whom JUSTICE O'CONNOR joins as to Part II, concurring in the judgment in part and dissenting in part.

I

Is respondent—who has tested positive for the human immunodeficiency virus (HIV) but was asymptomatic at the time she suffered discriminatory treatment—a person with a "disability" as that term is defined in the Americans with Disabilities Act of 1990(ADA)? * * *

It is important to note that whether respondent has a disability covered by the ADA is an individualized inquiry. The Act could not be clearer on this point: Section 12102(2) states explicitly that the disability determination must be made "with respect to an individual." Were this not sufficiently clear, the Act goes on to provide that the "major life activities" allegedly limited by an impairment must be those "of such individual." § 12102(3)(A).

The individualized nature of the inquiry is particularly important in this case because the District Court disposed of it on summary judgment. Thus all disputed issues of material fact must be resolved against respondent. She contends that her asymptomatic HIV status brings her within the first definition of a "disability." She must therefore demonstrate, inter alia, that she was (1) physically or mentally impaired and that such impairment (2) substantially limited (3) one or more of her major life activities.

Petitioner does not dispute that asymptomatic HIV-positive status is a physical impairment. I therefore assume this to be the case, and proceed to the second and third statutory requirements for "disability."

According to the Court, the next question is "whether reproduction is a major life activity." That, however, is only half of the relevant question. As mentioned above, the ADA's definition of a "disability" requires that the major life activity at issue be one "of such individual." The Court truncates the question, perhaps because there is not a shred of record evidence indicating that, prior to becoming infected with HIV, respondent's major life activities included reproduction (assuming for the moment that reproduction is a major life activity at all). At most, the record indicates that after learning of her HIV status, respondent, whatever her previous inclination, conclusively decided that she would not have children. There is absolutely no evidence that, absent the HIV, respondent would have had or was even considering having children. Indeed, when asked during her deposition whether her HIV infection had in any way impaired her ability to carry out any of her life functions, respondent answered "No." It is further telling that in the course of her entire brief to this Court, respondent studiously avoids asserting even once that reproduction is a major life activity to her. To the contrary, she argues that the "major life activity" inquiry should not turn on a particularized assessment of the circumstances of this or any other case.

But even aside from the facts of this particular case, the Court is simply wrong in concluding as a general matter that reproduction is a "major life activity." Unfortunately, the ADA does not define the phrase "major life activities." But the Act does incorporate by reference a list of such activities contained in regulations issued under the Rehabilitation Act. The Court correctly recognizes that this list of major life activities "is illustrative, not exhaustive," but then makes no attempt to demonstrate that reproduction is a major life activity in the same sense that "caring for one's self, performing manual tasks, walking, seeing, hearing, speaking, breathing, learning, and working" are.

Instead, the Court argues that reproduction is a "major" life activity in that it is "central to the life process itself." In support of this reading, the Court focuses on the fact that "major" indicates "comparative importance," ignoring the alternative definition of "major" as "greater in quantity, number, or extent." It is the latter definition that is most consistent with the ADA's illustrative list of major life activities.

No one can deny that reproductive decisions are important in a person's life. But so are decisions as to who to marry, where to live, and how to earn one's living. Fundamental importance of this sort is not the common thread linking the statute's listed activities. The common thread is rather that the activities are repetitively performed and essential in the day-to-day existence of a normally functioning individual. They are thus quite different from the series of activities leading to the birth of a child.

Both respondent and the United States as amicus curiae argue that reproduction must be a major life activity because regulations issued under the ADA define the term "physical impairment" to include physiological disorders affecting the reproductive system. If reproduction were not a major life activity, they argue, then it would have made little sense to include the reproductive disorders in the roster of physical impairments. This argument is simply wrong. There are numerous disorders of the reproductive system, such as dysmenorrhea and endometriosis, which are so painful that they limit a woman's ability to engage in major life activities such as walking and working. And, obviously, cancer of the various reproductive organs limits one's ability to engage in numerous activities other than reproduction.

But even if I were to assume that reproduction is a major life activity of respondent, I do not agree that an asymptomatic HIV infection "substantially limits" that activity. The record before us leaves no doubt that those so infected are still entirely able to engage in sexual intercourse, give birth to a child if they become pregnant, and perform the manual tasks necessary to rear a child to maturity. While individuals infected with HIV may choose not to engage in these activities, there is no support in language, logic, or our case law for the proposition that such voluntary choices constitute a "limit" on one's own life activities.

The Court responds that the ADA "addresses substantial limitations on major life activities, not utter inabilities." I agree, but fail to see how this assists the Court's cause. Apart from being unable to demonstrate that she is utterly unable to engage in the various activities that comprise the reproductive process, respondent has not even explained how she is less able to engage in those activities.

Respondent contends that her ability to reproduce is limited because "the fatal nature of HIV infection means that a parent is unlikely to live long enough to raise and nurture the child to adulthood." But the ADA's definition of a disability is met only if the alleged impairment substantially "limits" (present tense) a major life activity. Asymptomatic HIV does not presently limit respondent's ability to perform any of the tasks necessary to bear or raise a child. Respondent's argument, taken to its logical extreme, would render every individual with a genetic marker for some debilitating disease "disabled" here and now because of some possible future effects.

In my view, therefore, respondent has failed to demonstrate that any of her major life activities were substantially limited by her HIV infection.

II

While the Court concludes to the contrary as to the "disability" issue, it then quite correctly recognizes that petitioner could nonetheless have refused to treat respondent if her condition posed a "direct threat." The Court of Appeals affirmed the judgment of the District Court granting summary judgment to respondent on this issue. The Court vacates this portion of the Court of Appeals' decision, and remands the case to the lower court, presumably so that it may "determine whether our analysis of some of the studies cited by the parties would change its conclusion that petitioner presented neither objective evidence nor a triable issue of fact on the question of risk." I agree that the judgment should be vacated, although I am not sure I understand the Court's cryptic direction to the lower court.

"[D]irect threat" is defined as a "significant risk to the health or safety of others that cannot be eliminated by a modification of policies, practices, or procedures or by the provision of auxiliary aides or services." This statutory definition of a direct threat consists of two parts. First, a court must ask whether treating the infected patient without precautionary techniques would pose a "significant risk to the heath or safety of others." Whether a particular risk is significant depends on:

" "(a) the nature of the risk (how the disease is transmitted), (b) the duration of the risk (how long is the carrier infectious), (c) the severity of the risk (what is the potential harm to third parties) and (d) the probabilities the disease will be transmitted and will cause varying degrees of harm.' " School Bd. of Nassau Cty. v. Arline, 480 U.S. 273, 288, 107 S.Ct. 1123, 1131, 94 L.Ed.2d 307 (1987).

Even if a significant risk exists, a health practitioner will still be required to treat the infected patient if "a modification of policies, practices, or procedures" (in this case, universal precautions) will "eliminat [e]" the risk.

I agree with the Court that "the existence, or nonexistence, of a significant risk must be determined from the standpoint of the person who refuses the treatment or accommodation," as of the time that the decision refusing treatment is made. I disagree with the Court, however, that "[i]n assessing the reasonableness of petitioner's actions, the views of public health authorities ... are of special weight and authority." Those views are, of course, entitled to a presumption of validity when the actions of those authorities themselves are challenged in court, and even in disputes between private parties where Congress has committed that dispute to adjudication by a public health authority. But in litigation between private parties originating in the federal courts, I am aware of no provision of law or judicial practice that would require or permit courts to give some scientific views more credence than others simply because they have been endorsed by a politically appointed public health authority (such as the Surgeon General). In litigation of this latter sort, which is what we face here, the credentials of the scientists employed by the public health authority, and the soundness of their studies, must stand on their own. * * *

Applying these principles here, it is clear to me that petitioner has presented more than enough evidence to avoid summary judgment on the "direct threat" question. * * * At a minimum, petitioner's evidence was sufficient to create a triable issue on this question, and summary judgment was accordingly not appropriate.

JUSTICE O'CONNOR, concurring in the judgment in part and dissenting in part.

I agree with THE CHIEF JUSTICE that respondent's claim of disability should be evaluated on an individualized basis and that she has not proven that her asymptomatic HIV status substantially limited one or more of her major life activities. In my view, the act of giving birth to a child, while a very important part of the lives of many women, is not generally the same as the representative major life activities of all persons—"caring for one's self, performing manual tasks, walking, seeing, hearing, speaking, breathing, learning, and working"—listed in regulations relevant to the Americans with Disabilities Act of 1990. Based on that conclusion, there is no need to address whether other aspects of intimate or family relationships not raised in this case could constitute major life activities; nor is there reason to consider whether

HIV status would impose a substantial limitation on one's ability to reproduce if reproduction were a major life activity.

SUTTON v. UNITED AIRLINES, INC.

Supreme Court of the United States, 1999.
__ U.S. __, 119 S.Ct. 2139, __ L.Ed.2d __.

JUSTICE O'CONNOR delivered the opinion of the Court.

The Americans with Disabilities Act of 1990 (ADA or Act), prohibits certain employers from discriminating against individuals on the basis of their disabilities. Petitioners challenge the dismissal of their ADA action for failure to state a claim upon which relief can be granted. We conclude that the complaint was properly dismissed. In reaching that result, we hold that the determination of whether an individual is disabled should be made with reference to measures that mitigate the individual's impairment, including, in this instance, eyeglasses and contact lenses. In addition, we hold that petitioners failed to allege properly that respondent "regarded" them as having a disability within the meaning of the ADA.

I

Petitioners' amended complaint was dismissed for failure to state a claim upon which relief could be granted. Accordingly, we accept the allegations contained in their complaint as true for purposes of this case.

Petitioners are twin sisters, both of whom have severe myopia. Each petitioner's uncorrected visual acuity is 20/200 or worse in her right eye and 20/400 or worse in her left eye, but "[w]ith the use of corrective lenses, each ... has vision that is 20/20 or better." Consequently, without corrective lenses, each "effectively cannot see to conduct numerous activities such as driving a vehicle, watching television or shopping in public stores," but with corrective measures, such as glasses or contact lenses, both "function identically to individuals without a similar impairment."

In 1992, petitioners applied to respondent for employment as commercial airline pilots. They met respondent's basic age, education, experience, and FAA certification qualifications. After submitting their applications for employment, both petitioners were invited by respondent to an interview and to flight simulator tests. Both were told during their interviews, however, that a mistake had been made in inviting them to interview because petitioners did not meet respondent's minimum vision requirement, which was uncorrected visual acuity of 20/100 or better. Due to their failure to meet this requirement, petitioners' interviews were terminated, and neither was offered a pilot position.

In light of respondent's proffered reason for rejecting them, petitioners filed a charge of disability discrimination under the ADA with the Equal Employment Opportunity Commission (EEOC). After receiving a right to sue letter, petitioners filed suit in the United States District Court for the District of Colorado, alleging that respondent had discrimi-

DIST. CT.

nated against them "on the basis of their disability, or because [respondent] regarded [petitioners] as having a disability" in violation of the ADA. Specifically, petitioners alleged that due to their severe myopia they actually have a substantially limiting impairment or are regarded as having such an impairment, and are thus disabled under the Act.

The District Court dismissed petitioners' complaint for failure to state a claim upon which relief could be granted. Because petitioners could fully correct their visual impairments, the court held that they were not actually substantially limited in any major life activity and thus had not stated a claim that they were disabled within the meaning of the ADA. The court also determined that petitioners had not made allegations sufficient to support their claim that they were "regarded" by the respondent as having an impairment that substantially limits a major life activity. The court observed that "[t]he statutory reference to a substantial limitation indicates ... that an employer regards an employee as handicapped in his or her ability to work by finding the employee's impairment to foreclose generally the type of employment involved." But petitioners had alleged only that respondent regarded them as unable to satisfy the requirements of a particular job, global airline pilot. Consequently, the court held that petitioners had not stated a claim that they were regarded as substantially limited in the major life activity of working. Employing similar logic, the Court of Appeals for the Tenth Circuit affirmed the District Court's judgment.

The Tenth Circuit's decision is in tension with the decisions of other Courts of Appeals. We granted certiorari and now affirm.

II

The ADA prohibits discrimination by covered entities, including private employers, against qualified individuals with a disability. Specifically, it provides that no covered employer "shall discriminate against a qualified individual with a disability because of the disability of such individual in regard to job application procedures, the hiring, advancement, or discharge of employees, employee compensation, job training, and other terms, conditions, and privileges of employment." ("The term 'covered entity' means an employer, employment agency, labor organization, or joint labor-management committee"). A "qualified individual with a disability" is identified as "an individual with a disability who, with or without reasonable accommodation, can perform the essential functions of the employment position that such individual holds or desires." In turn, a "disability" is defined as:

"(A) a physical or mental <u>impairment</u> that <u>substantially limit</u>s one or more of the <u>major life activities</u> of such individual;

"(B) a record of such an impairment; or

"(C) being regarded as having such an impairment."

Accordingly, to fall within this definition one must have an actual disability (subsection (A)), have a record of a disability (subsection (B)), or be regarded as having one (subsection (C)).

* * *

III

* * * [W]e turn first to the question whether petitioners have stated *Subsection (A)* a claim under subsection (A) of the disability definition, that is, whether they have alleged that they possess a physical impairment that substantially limits them in one or more major life activities. Because petitioners allege that with corrective measures their vision "is 20/20 or better," they are not actually disabled within the meaning of the Act if the disability" determination is made with reference to these measures. Consequently, with respect to subsection (A) of the disability definition, our decision turns on whether disability is to be determined with or without reference to corrective measures.

Petitioners maintain that whether an impairment is substantially limiting should be determined without regard to corrective measures. They argue that, because the ADA does not directly address the question at hand, the Court should defer to the agency interpretations of the statute, which are embodied in the agency guidelines issued by the EEOC and the Department of Justice. These guidelines specifically direct that the determination of whether an individual is substantially limited in a major life activity be made without regard to mitigating measures.

Respondent, in turn, maintains that an impairment does not substantially limit a major life activity if it is corrected. It argues that the Court should not defer to the agency guidelines cited by petitioners because the guidelines conflict with the plain meaning of the ADA. The phrase "substantially limits one or more major life activities," it explains, requires that the substantial limitations actually and presently exist. Moreover, respondent argues, disregarding mitigating measures taken by an individual defies the statutory command to examine the effect of the impairment on the major life activities "of such individual." And even if the statute is ambiguous, respondent claims, the guidelines' directive to ignore mitigating measures is not reasonable, and thus this Court should not defer to it.

We conclude that respondent is correct that the approach adopted by the agency guidelines—that persons are to be evaluated in their hypothetical uncorrected state—is an impermissible interpretation of the ADA. Looking at the Act as a whole, it is apparent that if a person is taking measures to correct for, or mitigate, a physical or mental impairment, the effects of those measures—both positive and negative—must be taken into account when judging whether that person is "substantially limited" in a major life activity and thus "disabled" under the Act. The dissent relies on the legislative history of the ADA for the contrary proposition that individuals should be examined in their uncorrected state. Because we decide that, by its terms, the ADA cannot be read in this manner, we have no reason to consider the ADA's legislative history.

Three separate provisions of the ADA, read in concert, lead us to this conclusion. The Act defines a "disability" as "a physical or mental impairment that substantially limits one or more of the major life activities" of an individual. Because the phrase "substantially limits" appears in the Act in the present indicative verb form, we think the language is properly read as requiring that a person be presently—not potentially or hypothetically—substantially limited in order to demonstrate a disability. A "disability" exists only where an impairment "substantially limits" a major life activity, not where it "might," "could," or "would" be substantially limiting if mitigating measures were not taken. A person whose physical or mental impairment is corrected by medication or other measures does not have an impairment that presently "substantially limits" a major life activity. To be sure, a person whose physical or mental impairment is corrected by mitigating measures still has an impairment, but if the impairment is corrected it does not "substantially limi[t]" a major life activity.

The definition of disability also requires that disabilities be evaluated "with respect to an individual" and be determined based on whether an impairment substantially limits the "major life activities of such individual." Thus, whether a person has a disability under the ADA is an individualized inquiry. See Bragdon v. Abbott, 524 U.S. 624, ___, 118 S.Ct. 2196, 141 L.Ed.2d 540 (1998) (declining to consider whether HIV infection is a per se disability under the ADA).

The agency guidelines' directive that persons be judged in their uncorrected or unmitigated state runs directly counter to the individualized inquiry mandated by the ADA. The agency approach would often require courts and employers to speculate about a person's condition and would, in many cases, force them to make a disability determination based on general information about how an uncorrected impairment usually affects individuals, rather than on the individual's actual condition. For instance, under this view, courts would almost certainly find all diabetics to be disabled, because if they failed to monitor their blood sugar levels and administer insulin, they would almost certainly be substantially limited in one or more major life activities. A diabetic whose illness does not impair his or her daily activities would therefore be considered disabled simply because he or she has diabetes. Thus, the guidelines approach would create a system in which persons often must be treated as members of a group of people with similar impairments, rather than as individuals. This is contrary to both the letter and the spirit of the ADA.

The guidelines approach could also lead to the anomalous result that in determining whether an individual is disabled, courts and employers could not consider any negative side effects suffered by an individual resulting from the use of mitigating measures, even when those side effects are very severe. This result is also inconsistent with the individualized approach of the ADA.

Finally, and critically, findings enacted as part of the ADA require the conclusion that Congress did not intend to bring under the statute's protection all those whose uncorrected conditions amount to disabilities. Congress found that "some 43,000,000 Americans have one or more physical or mental disabilities, and this number is increasing as the population as a whole is growing older." § 12101(a)(1). This figure is inconsistent with the definition of disability pressed by petitioners.

Although the exact source of the 43 million figure is not clear, the corresponding finding in the 1988 precursor to the ADA was drawn directly from a report prepared by the National Council on Disability. * * * Regardless of its exact source, however, the 43 million figure reflects an understanding that those whose impairments are largely corrected by medication or other devices are not "disabled" within the meaning of the ADA.

By contrast, nonfunctional approaches to defining disability produce significantly larger numbers. * * * [T]he 1986 National Council on Disability report estimated that there were over 160 million disabled under the "health conditions approach."

Because it is included in the ADA's text, the finding that 43 million individuals are disabled gives content to the ADA's terms, specifically the term "disability." Had Congress intended to include all persons with corrected physical limitations among those covered by the Act, it undoubtedly would have cited a much higher number of disabled persons in the findings. That it did not is evidence that the ADA's coverage is restricted to only those whose impairments are not mitigated by corrective measures.

The dissents suggest that viewing individuals in their corrected state will exclude from the definition of "disab[led]" those who use prosthetic limbs, or take medicine for epilepsy or high blood pressure. This suggestion is incorrect. The use of a corrective device does not, by itself, relieve one's disability. Rather, one has a disability under subsection A if, notwithstanding the use of a corrective device, that individual is substantially limited in a major life activity. For example, individuals who use prosthetic limbs or wheelchairs may be mobile and capable of functioning in society but still be disabled because of a substantial limitation on their ability to walk or run. The same may be true of individuals who take medicine to lessen the symptoms of an impairment so that they can function but nevertheless remain substantially limited. Alternatively, one whose high blood pressure is "cured" by medication may be regarded as disabled by a covered entity, and thus disabled under subsection C of the definition. The use or nonuse of a corrective device does not determine whether an individual is disabled; that determination depends on whether the limitations an individual with an impairment actually faces are in fact substantially limiting.

Applying this reading of the Act to the case at hand, we conclude that the Court of Appeals correctly resolved the issue of disability in respondent's favor. As noted above, petitioners allege that with corrective measures, their visual acuity is 20/20 and that they "function identically to individuals without a similar impairment". In addition, petitioners concede that they "do not argue that the use of corrective lenses in itself demonstrates a substantially limiting impairment." Accordingly, because we decide that disability under the Act is to be determined with reference to corrective measures, we agree with the courts below that petitioners have not stated a claim that they are substantially limited in any major life activity.

IV

SubSection (C)

Our conclusion that petitioners have failed to state a claim that they are actually disabled under subsection (A) of the disability definition does not end our inquiry. Under subsection (C), individuals who are "regarded as" having a disability are disabled within the meaning of the ADA. See § 12102(2)(C). Subsection (C) provides that having a disability includes "being regarded as having a physical or mental impairment that substantially limits one or more of the major life activities of such individual," § 12102(2)(A). There are two apparent ways in which individuals may fall within this statutory definition: (1) a covered entity mistakenly believes that a person has a physical impairment that substantially limits one or more major life activities, or (2) a covered entity mistakenly believes that an actual, nonlimiting impairment substantially limits one or more major life activities. In both cases, it is necessary that a covered entity entertain misperceptions about the individual—it must believe either that one has a substantially limiting impairment that one does not have or that one has a substantially limiting impairment when, in fact, the impairment is not so limiting. These misperceptions often "resul[t] from stereotypic assumptions not truly indicative of . . . individual ability."

There is no dispute that petitioners are physically impaired. Petitioners do not make the obvious argument that they are regarded due to their impairments as substantially limited in the major life activity of seeing. They contend only that respondent mistakenly believes their physical impairments substantially limit them in the major life activity of working. To support this claim, petitioners allege that respondent has a vision requirement, which is allegedly based on myth and stereotype. Further, this requirement substantially limits their ability to engage in the major life activity of working by precluding them from obtaining the job of global airline pilot, which they argue is a "class of employment." In reply, respondent argues that the position of global airline pilot is not a class of jobs and therefore petitioners have not stated a claim that they are regarded as substantially limited in the major life activity of working.

Standing alone, the allegation that respondent has a vision requirement in place does not establish a claim that respondent regards petitioners as substantially limited in the major life activity of working. By its terms, the ADA allows employers to prefer some physical attributes over others and to establish physical criteria. An employer runs afoul of the ADA when it makes an employment decision based on a physical or mental impairment, real or imagined, that is regarded as substantially limiting a major life activity. Accordingly, an employer is free to decide that physical characteristics or medical conditions that do not rise to the level of an impairment—such as one's height, build, or singing voice— are preferable to others, just as it is free to decide that some limiting, but not substantially limiting, impairments make individuals less than ideally suited for a job.

Considering the allegations of the amended complaint in tandem, petitioners have not stated a claim that respondent regards their impairment as substantially limiting their ability to work. The ADA does not define "substantially limits," but "substantially" suggests "considerable" or "specified to a large degree." The EEOC has codified regulations interpreting the term "substantially limits" in this manner, defining the term to mean "[u]nable to perform" or "[s]ignificantly restricted." See 29 CFR §§ 1630.2(j)(1)(i), (ii) (1998)

When the major life activity under consideration is that of working, the statutory phrase "substantially limits" requires, at a minimum, that plaintiffs allege they are unable to work in a broad class of jobs. Reflecting this requirement, the EEOC uses a specialized definition of the term "substantially limits" when referring to the major life activity of working:

> "significantly restricted in the ability to perform either a class of jobs or a broad range of jobs in various classes as compared to the average person having comparable training, skills and abilities. The inability to perform a single, particular job does not constitute a substantial limitation in the major life activity of working." § 1630.2(j)(3)(i).

[margin handwritten note: EEOC. DEF. OF "SUBSTANTIAL LIMITS" → WORKING]

The EEOC further identifies several factors that courts should consider when determining whether an individual is substantially limited in the major life activity of working, including the geographical area to which the individual has reasonable access, and "the number and types of jobs utilizing similar training, knowledge, skills or abilities, within the geographical area, from which the individual is also disqualified." §§ 1630.2(j)(3)(ii)(A), (B). To be substantially limited in the major life activity of working, then, one must be precluded from more than one type of job, a specialized job, or a particular job of choice. If jobs utilizing an individual's skills (but perhaps not his or her unique talents) are available, one is not precluded from a substantial class of jobs. Similarly, if a host of different types of jobs are available, one is not precluded from a broad range of jobs.

Because the parties accept that the term "major life activities" includes working, we do not determine the validity of the cited regulations. We note, however, that there may be some conceptual difficulty in defining "major life activities" to include work, for it seems "to argue in a circle to say that if one is excluded, for instance, by reason of [an impairment, from working with others] ... then that exclusion constitutes an impairment, when the question you're asking is, whether the exclusion itself is by reason of handicap." Indeed, even the EEOC has expressed reluctance to define "major life activities" to include working and has suggested that working be viewed as a residual life activity, considered, as a last resort, only "[i]f an individual is not substantially limited with respect to any other major life activity."

Assuming without deciding that working is a major life activity and that the EEOC regulations interpreting the term "substantially limits" are reasonable, petitioners have failed to allege adequately that their poor eyesight is regarded as an impairment that substantially limits them in the major life activity of working. They allege only that respondent regards their poor vision as precluding them from holding positions as a "global airline pilot." Because the position of global airline pilot is a single job, this allegation does not support the claim that respondent regards petitioners as having a substantially limiting impairment. Indeed, there are a number of other positions utilizing petitioners' skills, such as regional pilot and pilot instructor to name a few, that are available to them. Even under the EEOC's Interpretative Guidance, to which petitioners ask us to defer, "an individual who cannot be a commercial airline pilot because of a minor vision impairment, but who can be a commercial airline co-pilot or a pilot for a courier service, would not be substantially limited in the major life activity of working." 29 CFR pt. 1630, App. § 1630.2.

Petitioners also argue that if one were to assume that a substantial number of airline carriers have similar vision requirements, they would be substantially limited in the major life activity of working. Even assuming for the sake of argument that the adoption of similar vision requirements by other carriers would represent a substantial limitation on the major life activity of working, the argument is nevertheless flawed. It is not enough to say that if the physical criteria of a single employer were imputed to all similar employers one would be regarded as substantially limited in the major life activity of working only as a result of this imputation. An otherwise valid job requirement, such as a height requirement, does not become invalid simply because it would limit a person's employment opportunities in a substantial way if it were adopted by a substantial number of employers. Because petitioners have not alleged, and cannot demonstrate, that respondent's vision requirement reflects a belief that petitioners' vision substantially limits them, we agree with the decision of the Court of Appeals affirming the dismissal of petitioners' claim that they are regarded as disabled.

For these reasons, the decision of the Court of Appeals for the Tenth Circuit is affirmed.

It is so ordered.

JUSTICE GINSBURG, concurring.

I agree that 42 U.S.C. § 12102(2)(A) does not reach the legions of people with correctable disabilities. The strongest clues to Congress' perception of the domain of the Americans with Disabilities Act (ADA), as I see it, are legislative findings that "some 43,000,000 Americans have one or more physical or mental disabilities," and that "individuals with disabilities are a discrete and insular minority," persons "subjected to a history of purposeful unequal treatment, and relegated to a position of political powerlessness in our society". These declarations are inconsistent with the enormously embracing definition of disability petitioners urge. As the Court demonstrates, the inclusion of correctable disabilities within the ADA's domain would extend the Act's coverage to far more than 43 million people. And persons whose uncorrected eyesight is poor, or who rely on daily medication for their well-being, can be found in every social and economic class; they do not cluster among the politically powerless, nor do they coalesce as historical victims of discrimination. In short, in no sensible way can one rank the large numbers of diverse individuals with corrected disabilities as a "discrete and insular minority." I do not mean to suggest that any of the constitutional presumptions or doctrines that may apply to "discrete and insular" minorities in other contexts are relevant here; there is no constitutional dimension to this case. Congress' use of the phrase, however, is a telling indication of its intent to restrict the ADA's coverage to a confined, and historically disadvantaged, class.

JUSTICE STEVENS, with whom JUSTICE BREYER joins, dissenting.

When it enacted the Americans with Disabilities Act in 1990, Congress certainly did not intend to require United Air Lines to hire unsafe or unqualified pilots. Nor, in all likelihood, did it view every person who wears glasses as a member of a "discrete and insular minority." Indeed, by reason of legislative myopia it may not have foreseen that its definition of "disability" might theoretically encompass, not just "some 43,000,000 Americans," but perhaps two or three times that number. Nevertheless, if we apply customary tools of statutory construction, it is quite clear that the threshold question whether an individual is "disabled" within the meaning of the Act—and, therefore, is entitled to the basic assurances that the Act affords—focuses on her past or present physical condition without regard to mitigation that has resulted from rehabilitation, self-improvement, prosthetic devices, or medication. One might reasonably argue that the general rule should not apply to an impairment that merely requires a nearsighted person to wear glasses. But I believe that, in order to be faithful to the remedial purpose of the Act, we should give it a generous, rather than a miserly, construction.

There are really two parts to the question of statutory construction presented by this case. The first question is whether the determination of disability for people that Congress unquestionably intended to cover should focus on their unmitigated or their mitigated condition. If the correct answer to that question is the one provided by eight of the nine Federal Courts of Appeals to address the issue and by all three of the Executive agencies that have issued regulations or interpretive bulletins construing the statute—namely, that the statute defines "disability" without regard to ameliorative measures—it would still be necessary to decide whether that general rule should be applied to what might be characterized as a "minor, trivial impairment." I shall therefore first consider impairments that Congress surely had in mind before turning to the special facts of this case.

I

"As in all cases of statutory construction, our task is to interpret the words of [the statute] in light of the purposes Congress sought to serve."

Congress expressly provided that the "purpose of [the ADA is] to provide a clear and comprehensive national mandate for the elimination of discrimination against individuals with disabilities." To that end, the ADA prohibits covered employers from "discriminat [ing] against a qualified individual with a disability because of the disability" in regard to the terms, conditions, and privileges of employment.

The Act's definition of disability is drawn "almost verbatim" from the Rehabilitation Act of 1973. The ADA's definition provides:

"The term 'disability' means, with respect to an individual—

"(A) a physical or mental impairment that substantially limits one or more of the major life activities of such individual;

"(B) a record of such an impairment; or

"(C) being regarded as having such an impairment." 42 U.S.C. § 12102(2).

The three parts of this definition do not identify mutually exclusive, discrete categories. On the contrary, they furnish three overlapping formulas aimed at ensuring that individuals who now have, or ever had, a substantially limiting impairment are covered by the Act.

An example of a rather common condition illustrates this point: There are many individuals who have lost one or more limbs in industrial accidents, or perhaps in the service of their country in places like Iwo Jima. With the aid of prostheses, coupled with courageous determination and physical therapy, many of these hardy individuals can perform all of their major life activities just as efficiently as an average couch potato. If the Act were just concerned with their present ability to participate in society, many of these individuals' physical impairments would not be viewed as disabilities. Similarly, if the statute were solely concerned with whether these individuals viewed themselves as disabled—or with whether a majority of employers regarded them as unable to perform most jobs—many of these individuals would lack statutory protection from discrimination based on their prostheses.

The sweep of the statute's three-pronged definition, however, makes it pellucidly clear that Congress intended the Act to cover such persons. The fact that a prosthetic device, such as an artificial leg, has restored one's ability to perform major life activities surely cannot mean that subsection (A) of the definition is inapplicable. Nor should the fact that the individual considers himself (or actually is) "cured," or that a prospective employer considers him generally employable, mean that subsections (B) or (C) are inapplicable. But under the Court's emphasis on "the present indicative verb form" used in subsection (A), that subsection presumably would not apply. And under the Court's focus on the individual's "presen[t]—not potentia[l] or hypothetica[l]"—condition, ibid., and on whether a person is "precluded from a broad range of jobs," subsections (B) and (C) presumably would not apply.

In my view, when an employer refuses to hire the individual "because of" his prosthesis, and the prosthesis in no way affects his ability to do the job, that employer has unquestionably discriminated against the individual in violation of the Act. Subsection (B) of the definition, in fact, sheds a revelatory light on the question whether Congress was concerned only about the corrected or mitigated status of a person's impairment. If the Court is correct that "[a] 'disability' exists only where" a person's "present" or "actual" condition is substantially impaired, there would be no reason to include in the protected class those who were once disabled but who are now fully recovered. Subsection (B) of the Act's definition, however, plainly covers a person who previously had a serious hearing impairment that has since been completely cured. Still, if I correctly understand the Court's opinion, it holds that one who continues to wear a hearing aid that she has worn all her life might not be covered—fully cured impairments are covered, but merely treatable ones are not. The text of the Act surely does not require such a bizarre result.

The three prongs of the statute, rather, are most plausibly read together not to inquire into whether a person is currently "functionally" limited in a major life activity, but only into the existence of an impairment—present or past—that substantially limits, or did so limit, the individual before amelioration. This reading avoids the counterintuitive conclusion that the ADA's safeguards vanish when individuals make themselves more employable by ascertaining ways to overcome their physical or mental limitations.

To the extent that there may be doubt concerning the meaning of the statutory text, ambiguity is easily removed by looking at the legislative history. * * * The Committee Reports on the bill that became the ADA make it abundantly clear that Congress intended the ADA to cover individuals who could perform all of their major life activities only with the help of ameliorative measures.

The ADA originated in the Senate. The Senate Report states that "whether a person has a disability should be assessed without regard to the availability of mitigating measures, such as reasonable accommodations or auxiliary aids." S.Rep. No. 101–116, p. 23 (1989). The Report further explained, in discussing the "regarded as" prong:

"[An] important goal of the third prong of the [disability] definition is to ensure that persons with medical conditions that are under control, and that therefore do not currently limit major life activities, are not discriminated against on the basis of their medical conditions. For example, individuals with controlled diabetes or epilepsy are often denied jobs for which they are qualified. Such denials are the result of negative attitudes and misinformation."

When the legislation was considered in the House of Representatives, its Committees reiterated the Senate's basic understanding of the Act's coverage, with one minor modification: They clarified that "correctable" or "controllable" disabilities were covered in the first definitional prong as well. The Report of the House Committee on the Judiciary states, in discussing the first prong, that, when determining whether an individual's impairment substantially limits a major life activity, "[t]he impairment should be assessed without considering whether mitigating measures, such as auxiliary aids or reasonable accommodations, would result in a less-than-substantial limitation." H.R.Rep. No. 101–485, pt. III, p. 28 (1990). The Report continues that "a person with epilepsy, an impairment which substantially limits a major life activity, is covered under this test," as is a person with poor hearing, "even if the hearing loss is corrected by the use of a hearing aid."

The Report of the House Committee on Education and Labor likewise states that "[w]hether a person has a disability should be assessed without regard to the availability of mitigating measures, such as reasonable accommodations or auxiliary aids." To make matters perfectly plain, the Report adds: "For example, a person who is hard of hearing is substantially limited in the major life activity of hearing, even though the loss may be corrected through the use of a hearing aid. Likewise, persons with impairments, such as epilepsy or diabetes, which substantially limit a major life activity are covered under the first prong of the definition of disability, even if the effects of the impairment are controlled by medication."

* * *

In addition, each of the three Executive agencies charged with implementing the Act has consistently interpreted the Act as mandating that the presence of disability turns on an individual's uncorrected state. We have traditionally accorded respect to such views when, as here, the agencies "played a pivotal role in setting [the statutory] machinery in motion."

The EEOC's Interpretive Guidance provides that "[t]he determination of whether an individual is substantially limited in a major life activity must be made on a case by case basis, without regard to mitigating measures such as medicines, or assistive or prosthetic devices." 29 CFR pt. 1630, App. § 1630.2(j) (1998). The EEOC further explains:

> "[A]n individual who uses artificial legs would ... be substantially limited in the major life activity of walking because the individual is unable to walk without the aid of prosthetic devices. Similarly, a diabetic who without insulin would lapse into a coma would be substantially limited because the individual cannot perform major life activities without the aid of medication."

The Department of Justice has reached the same conclusion. * * *

II

* * *

If a narrow reading of the term "disability" were necessary in order to avoid the danger that the Act might otherwise force United to hire pilots who might endanger the lives of their passengers, it would make good sense to use the "43,000,000 Americans" finding to confine its coverage. There is, however, no such danger in this case. If a person is "disabled" within the meaning of the Act, she still cannot prevail on a claim of discrimination unless she can prove that the employer took action "because of" that impairment, and that she can, "with or without reasonable accommodation, . . . perform the essential functions" of the job of a commercial airline pilot. Even then, an employer may avoid liability if it shows that the criteria of having uncorrected visual acuity of at least 20/100 is "job-related and consistent with business necessity" or if such vision (even if correctable to 20/20) would pose a health or safety hazard.

This case, in other words, is not about whether petitioners are genuinely qualified or whether they can perform the job of an airline pilot without posing an undue safety risk. The case just raises the threshold question whether petitioners are members of the ADA's protected class. It simply asks whether the ADA lets petitioners in the door in the same way as the Age Discrimination in Employment Act of 1967 does for every person who is at least 40 years old and as Title VII of the Civil Rights Act of 1964 does for every single individual in the work force. Inside that door lies nothing more than basic protection from irrational and unjustified discrimination because of a characteristic that is beyond a person's control. Hence, this particular case, at its core, is about whether, assuming that petitioners can prove that they are "qualified," the airline has any duty to come forward with some legitimate explanation for refusing to hire them because of their uncorrected eyesight, or whether the ADA leaves the airline free to decline to hire petitioners on this basis even if it is acting purely on the basis of irrational fear and stereotype.

I think it quite wrong for the Court to confine the coverage of the Act simply because an interpretation of "disability" that adheres to Congress' method of defining the class it intended to benefit may also provide protection for "significantly larger numbers" of individuals than estimated in the Act's findings. It has long been a "familiar canon of statutory construction that remedial legislation should be construed broadly to effectuate its purposes." Congress sought, in enacting the ADA, to "provide a . . . comprehensive national mandate for the discrimination against individuals with disabilities." The ADA, following the lead of the Rehabilitation Act before it, seeks to implement this mandate by encouraging employers "to replace . . . reflexive reactions to actual or perceived handicaps with actions based on medically sound judgments." Even if an authorized agency could interpret this statutory structure so as to pick and choose certain correctable impairments that Congress meant to exclude from this mandate, Congress surely has not authorized us to do so.

When faced with classes of individuals or types of discrimination that fall outside the core prohibitions of anti-discrimination statutes, we have consistently construed those statutes to include comparable evils within their coverage, even when the particular evil at issue was beyond Congress' immediate concern in passing the legislation. Congress, for instance, focused almost entirely on the problem of discrimination against African–Americans when it enacted Title VII of the Civil Rights Act of 1964. But that narrow focus could not possibly justify a construction of the statute that excluded Hispanic–Americans or Asian–Americans from its protection—or as we later decided (ironically enough, by relying on legislative history and according "great deference" to the EEOC's "interpretation"), Caucasians.

We unanimously applied this well-accepted method of interpretation last Term with respect to construing Title VII to cover claims of same-sex sexual harassment. Oncale v. Sundowner Offshore Services, Inc., 523 U.S. 75, 118 S.Ct. 998, 140 L.Ed.2d 201 (1998). We explained our holding as follows:

> "As some courts have observed, male-on-male sexual harassment in the workplace was assuredly not the principal evil Congress was concerned with when it enacted Title VII. But statutory prohibitions often go beyond the principal evil to cover reasonably comparable evils, and it is ultimately the provisions of our laws rather than the principal concerns of our legislators by which we are governed. Title VII prohibits 'discriminat[ion] ... because of ... sex' in the 'terms' or 'conditions' of employment. Our holding that this includes sexual harassment must extend to sexual harassment of any kind that meets the statutory requirements."

* * * Under the approach we followed in Oncale * * * visual impairments should be judged by the same standard as hearing impairments or any other medically controllable condition. The nature of the discrimination alleged is of the same character and should be treated accordingly.

* * *

I do not mean to suggest, of course, that the ADA should be read to prohibit discrimination on the basis of, say, blue eyes, deformed fingernails, or heights of less than six feet. Those conditions, to the extent that they are even "impairments," do not substantially limit individuals in any condition and thus are different in kind from the impairment in the case before us. While not all eyesight that can be enhanced by glasses is substantially limiting, having 20/200 vision in one's better eye is, without treatment, a significant hindrance. Only two percent of the population suffers from such myopia. Such acuity precludes a person from driving, shopping in a public store, or viewing a computer screen from a reasonable distance. Uncorrected vision, therefore, can be "substantially limiting" in the same way that unmedicated epilepsy or diabetes can be. Because Congress obviously intended to include individuals with the latter impairments in the Act's protected class, we should give petitioners the same protection.

III

The Court does not disagree that the logic of the ADA requires petitioner's visual impairment to be judged the same as other "correctable'' conditions. Instead of including petitioners within the Act's umbrella, however, the Court decides, in this opinion and its companion, to expel all individuals who, by using "measures [to] mitigate [their] impairment[s]" are able to overcome substantial limitations regarding major life activities. The Court, for instance, holds that severe hypertension that is substantially limiting without medication is not a "disability," Murphy v. United Parcel Service, Inc., and—perhaps even more remarkably—indicates (directly contrary to the Act's legislative history, that diabetes that is controlled only with insulin treatments is not a "disability" either.

The Court claims that this rule is necessary to avoid requiring courts to "speculate" about a person's "hypothetical" condition and to preserve the Act's focus on making "individualized inquiries" into whether a person is disabled. The Court also asserts that its rejection of the general rule of viewing individuals in their unmitigated state prevents distorting the scope of the Act's protected class to cover a "much higher number" of persons than Congress estimated in its findings. And, I suspect, the Court has been cowed by respondent's persistent argument that viewing all individuals in their unmitigated state will lead to a tidal wave of lawsuits. None of the Court's reasoning, however, justifies a construction of the Act that will obviously deprive many of Congress' intended beneficiaries of the legal protection it affords.

The agencies' approach, the Court repeatedly contends, "would create a system in which persons often must be treated as members of a group of people with similar impairments, rather than individuals, [which] is both contrary to the letter and spirit of the ADA." The Court's mantra regarding the Act's "individualized approach," however, fails to support its holding. I agree that the letter and spirit of the ADA is designed to deter decision making based on group stereotypes, but the agencies' interpretation of the Act does not lead to this result. Nor does it require courts to "speculate" about people's "hypothetical" conditions. Viewing a person in her "unmitigated" state simply requires examining that individual's abilities in a different state, not the abilities of every person who shares a similar condition. It is just as easy individually to test petitioners' eyesight with their glasses on as with their glasses off.

> Ironically, it is the Court's approach that actually condones treating individuals merely as members of groups. That misdirected approach permits any employer to dismiss out of hand every person who has uncorrected eyesight worse than 20/100 without regard to the specific qualifications of those individuals or the extent of their abilities to overcome their impairment. In much the same way, the Court's approach would seem to allow an employer to refuse to hire every person who has epilepsy or diabetes that is controlled by medication, or every person who functions efficiently with a prosthetic limb.

Under the Court's reasoning, an employer apparently could not refuse to hire persons with these impairments who are substantially limited even with medication, but that group-based "exception" is more perverse still. Since the purpose of the ADA is to dismantle employment barriers based on society's accumulated myths and fears, it is especially ironic to deny protection for persons with substantially limiting impairments that, when corrected, render them fully able and employable. Insofar as the Court assumes that the majority of individuals with impairments such as prosthetic limbs or epilepsy will still be covered under its approach because they are substantially limited "notwithstanding the use of a corrective device," I respectfully disagree as an empirical matter. Although it is of course true that some of these individuals are substantially limited in any condition, Congress enacted the ADA in part because such individuals are not ordinarily substantially limited in their mitigated condition, but rather are often the victims of "stereotypic assumptions not truly indicative of the individual ability of such individuals to participate in, and contribute to, society."

It has also been suggested that if we treat as "disabilities" impairments that may be mitigated by measures as ordinary and expedient as wearing eyeglasses, a flood of litigation will ensue. The suggestion is misguided. Although vision is of critical importance for airline pilots, in most segments of the economy whether an employee wears glasses—or uses any of several other mitigating measures—is a matter of complete indifference to employers. It is difficult to envision many situations in which a qualified employee who needs glasses to perform her job might be fired—as the statute requires—"because of" the fact that she cannot see well without them. Such a proposition would be ridiculous in the garden-variety case. On the other hand, if an accounting firm, for example, adopted a guideline refusing to hire any incoming accountant who has uncorrected vision of less than 20/100—or, by the same token, any person who is unable without medication to avoid having seizures— such a rule would seem to be the essence of invidious discrimination.

* * *

In the end, the Court is left only with its tenacious grip on Congress' finding that "some 43,000,000 Americans have one or more physical or mental disabilities"—and that figure's legislative history extrapolated from a law review "article authored by the drafter of the original ADA bill introduced in Congress in 1988." We previously have observed that a "statement of congressional findings is a rather thin reed upon which to base" a statutory construction. * * * It is equally undeniable, however, that "43 million" is not a fixed cap on the Act's protected class: By including the "record of" and "regarded as" categories, Congress fully expected the Act to protect individuals who lack, in the Court's words, "actual" disabilities, and therefore are not counted in that number.

* * *

Accordingly, although I express no opinion on the ultimate merits of petitioners' claim, I am persuaded that they have a disability covered by the ADA. I therefore respectfully dissent.

JUSTICE BREYER, dissenting.

We must draw a statutory line that either (1) will include within the category of persons authorized to bring suit under the Americans with Disabilities Act of 1990 some whom Congress may not have wanted to protect (those who wear ordinary eyeglasses), or (2) will exclude from the threshold category those whom Congress certainly did want to protect (those who successfully use corrective devices or medicines, such as hearing aids or prostheses or medicine for epilepsy). Faced with this dilemma, the statute's language, structure, basic purposes, and history require us to choose the former statutory line, as JUSTICE STEVENS (whose opinion I join) well explains. I would add that, if the more generous choice of threshold led to too many lawsuits that ultimately proved without merit or otherwise drew too much time and attention away from those whom Congress clearly sought to protect, there is a remedy. The Equal Employment Opportunity Commission (EEOC), through regulation, might draw finer definitional lines, excluding some of those who wear eyeglasses (say, those with certain vision impairments who readily can find corrective lenses), thereby cabining the overly broad extension of the statute that the majority fears.

* * *

Notes

1.   There were two companions to the principal case: *Albertsons, Inc v. Kirkingburg*, ___ U.S. ___, 119 S.Ct. 2162, ___ L.Ed.2d ___ (1999) and *Murphy v. United Parcel Service, Inc.*, ___ U.S. ___, 119 S.Ct. 2133, ___ L.Ed. ___ (1999).

a.   In *Albertsons*, the plaintiff suffered from an uncorrectable condition that left him with 20/200 vision in one eye. The consequence was that plaintiff had monocular vision. Seeing with one eye, rather than two, inevitably leads to some loss of horizontal field of vision and reduced depth perception. Plaintiff was dismissed from his truckdriver job with Albertsons because he failed to meet the Department of Transportation's basic vision standards for commercial truckdrivers. (Even though the DOT regulations allow for a waiver that plaintiff could have secured). The Ninth Circuit had concluded that plaintiff was an individual with a disability. The Court reversed. First, the Court reasoned that merely because there is a difference between the manner in which plaintiff sees and the manner in which most people will not itself transform plaintiff's condition into a disability. Second, as *Sutton* directed courts to consider mitigating measures, the lower court failed to recognize that the plaintiff's own brain, (rather than mechanical devices or medicine) had developed mechanisms for coping with and mitigating his visual impairment to the point that plaintiff was not in fact substantially limited in a major life activity. The Court re-emphasized that individuals must be evaluated a case-by-case basis, evaluating their own unique ability to perform major life functions. Depending on their own ability to mitigate the effect of the condition, persons with monocular vision often will be disabled. But the fact that many such persons will be substantially limited in the performance of major life activities, does not relieve this plaintiff from the burden of proving that he was so limited.

The Court proceeded to address a second issue raised by the employer, which is whether plaintiff was "qualified" for the position. According to the employer, even if plaintiff could establish that he was an individual with a disability, the fact that he did not satisfy the Department of Transportation's basic vision standards for the job he was holding rendered plaintiff unqualified for the position. Plaintiff countered that the waiver provisions of the federal regulations allowed past accident-free performance of a sight impaired driver to be the basis for a temporary waiver. As plaintiff had been successfully and safely performing this job for Albertsons, this would not only established that plaintiff was "qualified," but further, because of plaintiff's past performance that would permit a waiver, the employer must accept that plaintiff was qualified and cannot assert the basic governmental regulation as a qualification that plaintiff was unable to meet. The Court rejected plaintiff's argument, and held that an employer was free to establish the basic governmental standard as a qualification for the job, thus leaving plaintiff unable to prove that he was "qualified."

b.   In *Murphy* the plaintiff suffered from high blood pressure (hypertension). Although classified as a "mechanic" plaintiff was required to drive his employer's commercial vehicles. UPS fired plaintiff because plaintiff's untreated hypertension exceeded the levels set by the U.S. Department of Transportation for commercial vehicle drivers. With medication plaintiff's hypertension did not significantly restrict plaintiff's daily activities, and he could function normally and engage in activities other persons normally do. Relying on *Sutton* the Court concluded that plaintiff was not an "individual with a disability." The more difficult issue was whether plaintiff Murphy was "regarded as" having a disability by UPS, his employer. The Court viewed the situation thus: "Petition was fired from the position of a UPS mechanic because he has a physical impairment—hypertension—that is regarded as preventing him from obtaining DOT health certification. At most, petitioner has shown that he is regarded as unable to perform the job of mechanic only when that job requires driving a commercial motor vehicle—a specific type of vehicle used on a highway in interstate commerce. * * * Consequently, in light of petitioner's skills and the array of jobs available to petitioner utilizing those skills, petitioner has failed to show that he is regarded as unable to perform a class of jobs. Rather, the undisputed record evidence demonstrates that petitioner is, at most, regarded has unable to perform only a particular job. This is insufficient, as a matter of law, to prove that petitioner is regarded as substantially limited in the major life activity of working."

Chapter 19

AGE DISCRIMINATION

A. THE SUBSTANTIVE PROHIBITIONS: THE MEANING OF "AGE"

1. THE PROTECTED, "OVER 40," AGE CLASS

Page 619: AGE DISCRIMINATION

Review O'Connor v. Consolidated Coin Caterers Corp. reproduced, supra, in this supplement (517 U.S. 308, 116 S.Ct. 1307, 134 L.Ed.2d 433 (1996). The Court discussed the "protected class" of over age 40 concluding. "This language does not ban discrimination against employees because they are aged 40 or older; it bans discrimination against employees because of their age, but limits the protected class to those who are 40 or older. The fact that one person in the protected class has lost out to another person in the protected class is thus irrelevant, so long as he has lost out because of his age."

Question: Does this reasoning undermine the reasoning in the principal case in the text, page 615, *Hamilton v. Caterpillar, Inc.*?

The O'Connor Court went on to discuss the application of the *McDonnell Douglas* model to create an initial inference of illegally motivated age discrimination, concluding: "[T]he fact that an ADEA plaintiff was replaced by someone outside the protected class is not a proper element of the McDonnell Douglas prima facie case." The inference is created by demonstration that a replacement for plaintiff was "substantially younger" than the plaintiff.

PAGE 642: Note 5

The Higher Education Amendments of 1998 specifically allow institutions of higher education to offer tenured faculty members voluntary, age-based retirement through "supplemental benefits upon voluntary retirement that are reduced or eliminated on the basis of age." The additional benefits must be in addition to other retirement benefits that are offered to faculty members with similar contracts. The amendment will be codified at 29 U.S.C.A. 632(m).

B. THE DEFENSES

2. BONA FIDE EMPLOYEE BENEFIT PLANS

Page 644: Note 2

Oubre v. Entergy Operations, 522 U.S. 422, 118 S.Ct. 838, 139 L.Ed.2d 849 (1998) resolved the division of authority outlined in the note. Plaintiff/employee signed a release of claims that did not comply with 29 U.S.C.A. 626(f) in at least three particulars: (1) it did not provide the employee with sufficient time to consider options, (2) it did not allow seven days to revoke, and (3) the release did not specifically refer to possible Age Act claims. As part of the termination and waiver agreements the employee was promised and received significant severance payments from the employer. After the employer had made the last severance payment, the employee filed suit under the ADEA. The plaintiff/employee neither returned nor offered to return the severance payments he had received. The Court rejected the employer's argument that acceptance of the severance payments ratified the otherwise defective release. The Court reasoned that many former employees will lack funds to repay the employer, and thus would not be able to challenge illegal discrimination. This would frustrate the remedial purposes of the Act. The Court was also concerned that unscrupulous employers might offer releases that do not satisfy the safe harbor provisions of the statute with the expectation that employees would be unable to repay the consideration given for the defective release.

Part VII

PROCEDURES AND REMEDIES

Chapter 22

PROCEDURES, TIME LIMITATIONS, AND ADMINISTRATIVE PREREQUISITES TO SUIT

F. ALTERNATIVE FORUMS AND PRECLUSION

4. PRIOR ARBITRATION AWARDS

Page 742:

The tension between *Alexander v. Gardner–Denver* (S.Ct. 1974) and *Gilmer v. Interstate/Johnson Lane Corp.* (S.Ct. 1991) was addressed but not significantly relieved by **WRIGHT v. UNIVERSAL MARITIME SERVICE CORP.**, 525 U.S. 70, 119 S.Ct. 391, 142 L.Ed.2d 361 (1998). Speaking for a unanimous Court, Justice Scalia reasoned:

"In this case, the Fourth Circuit concluded that the general arbitration provision in the CBA [collective bargaining agreement] governing Wright's employment was sufficiently broad to encompass a statutory claim arising under the ADA, and that such a provision was enforceable. The latter conclusion brings into question two lines of our case law. The first is represented by Alexander v. Gardner–Denver Co., 415 U.S. 36, 94 S.Ct. 1011, 39 L.Ed.2d 147 (1974), which held that an employee does not forfeit his right to a judicial forum for claimed discriminatory discharge in violation of Title VII of the Civil Rights Act of 1964 if 'he first pursues his grievance to final arbitration under the nondiscrimination clause of a collective-bargaining agreement.' In rejecting the argument that the doctrine of election of remedies barred the Title VII lawsuit, we reasoned that a grievance is designed to vindicate a 'contractual right' under a CBA, while a lawsuit under Title VII asserts 'independent statutory rights accorded by Congress.' The statutory cause of action was not waived by the union's agreement to the arbitration provision of the CBA, since 'there can be no prospective waiver of an employee's rights under Title VII.' We have followed the holding of Gardner–

Denver in deciding the effect of CBA arbitration upon employee claims under other statutes.

"The second line of cases implicated here is represented by Gilmer v. Interstate/Johnson Lane Corp., supra, which held that a claim brought under the Age Discrimination in Employment Act of 1967 (ADEA), could be subject to compulsory arbitration pursuant to an arbitration provision in a securities registration form. Relying upon the federal policy favoring arbitration embodied in the Federal Arbitration Act (FAA) we said that 'statutory claims may be the subject of an arbitration agreement, enforceable pursuant to the FAA.'

"There is obviously some tension between these two lines of cases. Whereas Gardner–Denver stated that 'an employee's rights under Title VII are not susceptible of prospective waiver,' Gilmer held that the right to a federal judicial forum for an ADEA claim could be waived. Petitioner and the United States as amicus would have us reconcile the lines of authority by maintaining that federal forum rights cannot be waived in union-negotiated CBAs even if they can be waived in individually executed contracts—a distinction that assuredly finds support in the text of Gilmer. Respondents and their amici, on the other hand, contend that the real difference between Gardner–Denver and Gilmer is the radical change, over two decades, in the Court's receptivity to arbitration, leading Gilmer to affirm that 'questions of arbitrability must be addressed with a healthy regard for the federal policy favoring arbitration,' Gilmer, they argue, has sufficiently undermined Gardner–Denver that a union can waive employees' rights to a judicial forum. Although, as will appear, we find Gardner–Denver and Gilmer relevant for various purposes to the case before us, we find it unnecessary to resolve the question of the validity of a union-negotiated waiver, since it is apparent to us, on the facts and arguments presented here, that no such waiver has occurred.

"In asserting the existence of an agreement to arbitrate the ADA claim, respondents rely upon the presumption of arbitrability this Court has found in § 301 of the Labor Management Relations Act, 1947. In collective bargaining agreements, we have said, 'there is a presumption of arbitrability in the sense that '[a]n order to arbitrate the particular grievance should not be denied unless it may be said with positive assurance that the arbitration clause is not susceptible of an interpretation that covers the asserted dispute.'

"That presumption, however, does not extend beyond the reach of the principal rationale that justifies it, which is that arbitrators are in a better position than courts to interpret the terms of a CBA. This rationale finds support in the very text of the LMRA, which announces that '[f]inal adjustment by a method agreed upon by the parties is declared to be the desirable method for settlement of grievance disputes arising over the application or interpretation of an existing collective bargaining agreement. The dispute in the present case, however, ultimately concerns not the application or interpretation of any CBA, but the meaning of a federal statute. The cause of action Wright asserts arises not out of contract, but out of the ADA, and is distinct from any right conferred by the collective-bargaining agreement. To be sure, respondents argue that Wright is not qualified for his position as the CBA requires, but even if that were true he would still prevail if the refusal to hire violated the ADA.

"Nor is the statutory (as opposed to contractual) focus of the claim altered by the fact that Clause 17 of the CBA recites it to be 'the intention and purpose of all parties hereto that no provision or part of this Agreement shall be violative of any Federal or State Law.' As we discuss below in Part IV, this does not incorporate the ADA by reference. Even if it did so, however—thereby creating a contractual right that is coextensive with the federal statutory right—the ultimate question for the arbitrator would be not what the parties have agreed to, but what federal law requires; and that is not a question which should be presumed to be included within the arbitration requirement. Application of that principle is unaffected by the fact that the CBA in this case, unlike the one in Gardner–Denver, does not expressly limit the arbitrator to interpreting and applying the contract. The presumption only extends that far, whether or not the text of the agreement is similarly limited. It may well be that ordinary textual analysis of a CBA will show that matters which go beyond the interpretation and application of contract terms are subject to arbitration; but they will not be presumed to be so.

"Not only is petitioner's statutory claim not subject to a presumption of arbitrability; we think any CBA requirement to arbitrate it must be particularly clear. In Metropolitan Edison Co. v. NLRB, 460 U.S. 693, 103 S.Ct. 1467, 75 L.Ed.2d 387 (1983), we stated that a union could waive its officers' statutory right under § 8(a)(3) of the National Labor Relations Act to be free of antiunion discrimination, but we held that such a waiver must be clear and unmistakable. '[W]e will not infer from a general contractual provision that the parties intended to waive a statutorily protected right unless the undertaking is "explicitly stated." More succinctly, the waiver must be 'clear and unmistakable.'

"We think the same standard applicable to a union-negotiated waiver of employees' statutory right to a judicial forum for claims of employment discrimination. Although that is not a substantive right, and whether or not Gardner-Denver's seemingly absolute prohibition of union waiver of employees' federal forum rights survives Gilmer, Gardner–Denver at least stands for the proposition that the right to a federal judicial forum is of sufficient importance to be protected against less-than-explicit union waiver in a CBA. The

CBA in this case does not meet that standard. Its arbitration clause is very general, providing for arbitration of '[m]atters under dispute,' which could be understood to mean matters in dispute under the contract. And the remainder of the contract contains no explicit incorporation of statutory antidiscrimination requirements. (Indeed, it does not even contain, as did the CBAs in Austin and Gardner–Denver, its own specific antidiscrimination provision.) The Fourth Circuit relied upon the fact that the equivalently broad arbitration clause in Gilmer—applying to 'any dispute, claim or controversy'—was held to embrace federal statutory claims. But Gilmer involved an individual's waiver of his own rights, rather than a union's waiver of the rights of represented employees—and hence the 'clear and unmistakable' standard was not applicable.

"Respondents rely upon Clause 15(F) of the CBA, which states that 'this Agreement is intended to cover all matters affecting wages, hours, and other terms and conditions of employment.' But even if this could, in isolation, be considered a clear and unmistakable incorporation of employment-discrimination laws (which is doubtful), it is surely deprived of that effect by the provision, later in the same paragraph, that '[a]nything not contained in this Agreement shall not be construed as being part of this Agreement.' Respondents also rely upon Clause 17 of the CBA, which states that '[i]t is the intention and purpose of all parties hereto that no provision or part of this Agreement shall be violative of any Federal or State Law.' They argue that this requires the arbitrator to 'apply legal definitions derived from the ADA' in determining whether Wright is 'qualified' for employment within the meaning of the CBA. Brief for Respondents 39. Perhaps so, but that is not the same as making compliance with the ADA a contractual commitment that would be subject to the arbitration clause. This becomes crystal clear when one contrasts Clause 17 with the provision of the CBA which states that '[t]he requirements of the Occupations [sic] Safety and Health Administration shall be binding on both Parties.' (Under respondents' interpretation of Clause 17, this OSHA provision would be superfluous.) Clause 17 seems to us nothing more than a recitation of the canon of construction which would in any event have been applied to the CBA—that an agreement should be interpreted in such fashion as to preserve, rather than destroy, its validity (ut res magis valeat quam pereat).

"Finally, we do not find a clear and unmistakable waiver in the Longshore Seniority Plan. Like the CBA itself, the Plan contains no antidiscrimination provision; and it specifically limits its grievance procedure to disputes related to the agreement."

The Court therefore held that arbitration was not mandatory because the collective-bargaining agreement did not contain a 'clear and unmistakable waiver, of the covered employees' rights to a judicial forum for federal claims of employment discrimination. The Court failed to reach the question whether such a waiver would be enforceable.

————

Note: In a far reaching opinion the Ninth Circuit has held that employees may not be compelled as a condition of employment to waive their individual right to a judicial forum to resolve Title VII claims. *Duffield v. Robertson Stephens & Co.*, 144 F.3d 1182 (9th Cir. 1998).

Chapter 23

REMEDIES

C. DAMAGES

1. TITLE VII, § 1981, AND THE AMERICANS WITH DISABILITIES ACT

Page 759: Determining Malice or Reckless Disregard

KOLSTAD v. AMERICAN DENTAL ASSOCIATION

Supreme Court of the United States, 1999.
___ U.S. ___, 119 S.Ct. 2118, ___ L.Ed.2d ___.

JUSTICE O'CONNOR delivered the opinion of the Court.

Under the terms of the Civil Rights Act of 1991 punitive damages are available in claims under Title VII of the Civil Rights Act of 1964 and the Americans with Disabilities Act of 1990. Punitive damages are limited, however, to cases in which the employer has engaged in intentional discrimination and has done so "with malice or with reckless indifference to the federally protected rights of an aggrieved individual." 42 U.S.C. § 1981a(b)(1). We here consider the circumstances under which punitive damages may be awarded in an action under Title VII.

I

A

In September 1992, Jack O'Donnell announced that he would be retiring as the Director of Legislation and Legislative Policy and Director of the Council on Government Affairs and Federal Dental Services for respondent, American Dental Association (respondent or Association). Petitioner, Carole Kolstad, was employed with O'Donnell in respondent's Washington, D.C., office, where she was serving as respondent's Director of Federal Agency Relations. When she learned of O'Donnell's retirement, she expressed an interest in filling his position. Also interested in replacing O'Donnell was Tom Spangler, another employee in respondent's Washington office. At this time, Spangler was serving as the Association's Legislative Counsel, a position that involved him in respondent's legislative lobbying efforts. Both petitioner and Spangler had

71

worked directly with O'Donnell, and both had received "distinguished" performance ratings by the acting head of the Washington office, Leonard Wheat.

Both petitioner and Spangler formally applied for O'Donnell's position, and Wheat requested that Dr. William Allen, then serving as respondent's Executive Director in the Association's Chicago office, make the ultimate promotion decision. After interviewing both petitioner and Spangler, Wheat recommended that Allen select Spangler for O'Donnell's post. Allen notified petitioner in December 1992 that he had, in fact, selected Spangler to serve as O'Donnell's replacement. Petitioner's challenge to this employment decision forms the basis of the instant action.

B

After first exhausting her avenues for relief before the Equal Employment Opportunity Commission, petitioner filed suit against the Association in Federal District Court, alleging that respondent's decision to promote Spangler was an act of employment discrimination proscribed under Title VII. In petitioner's view, the entire selection process was a sham. Counsel for petitioner urged the jury to conclude that Allen's stated reasons for selecting Spangler were pretext for gender discrimination, and that Spangler had been chosen for the position before the formal selection process began. Among the evidence offered in support of this view, there was testimony to the effect that Allen modified the description of O'Donnell's post to track aspects of the job description used to hire Spangler. In petitioner's view, this "preselection" procedure suggested an intent by the Association to discriminate on the basis of sex. Petitioner also introduced testimony at trial that Wheat told sexually offensive jokes and that he had referred to certain prominent professional women in derogatory terms. Moreover, Wheat allegedly refused to meet with petitioner for several weeks regarding her interest in O'Donnell's position. Petitioner testified, in fact, that she had historically experienced difficulty gaining access to meet with Wheat. Allen, for his part, testified that he conducted informal meetings regarding O'Donnell's position with both petitioner and Spangler, although petitioner stated that Allen did not discuss the position with her.

The District Court denied petitioner's request for a jury instruction on punitive damages. The jury concluded that respondent had discriminated against petitioner on the basis of sex and awarded her backpay totaling $52,718. Although the District Court subsequently denied respondent's motion for judgment as a matter of law on the issue of liability, the court made clear that it had not been persuaded that respondent had selected Spangler over petitioner on the basis of sex, and the court denied petitioner's requests for reinstatement and for attorney's fees.

Petitioner appealed from the District Court's decisions denying her requested jury instruction on punitive damages and her request for reinstatement and attorney's fees. Respondent cross-appealed from the denial of its motion for judgment as a matter of law. In a split decision, a panel of the Court of Appeals for the District of Columbia Circuit reversed the District Court's decision denying petitioner's request for an instruction on punitive damages. In so doing, the court rejected respondent's claim that punitive damages are available under Title VII only in " 'extraordinarily egregious cases.' " The panel reasoned that, "because 'the state of mind necessary to trigger liability for the wrong is at least as culpable as that required to make punitive damages applicable,' " the fact that the jury could reasonably have found intentional discrimination meant that the jury should have been permitted to consider punitive damages. The court noted, however, that not all cases involving intentional discrimination would support a punitive damages award. Such an award might be improper, the panel reasoned, in instances where the employer justifiably believes that intentional discrimination is permitted or where an employee engages in discrimination outside the scope of that employee's authority. Here, the court concluded, respondent "neither attempted to justify the use of sex in its promotion decision nor disavowed the actions of its agents."

The Court of Appeals subsequently agreed to rehear the case en banc, limited to the punitive damages question. In a divided opinion, the court affirmed the decision of the District Court. The en banc majority concluded that, "before the question of punitive damages can go to the jury, the evidence of the defendant's culpability must exceed what is needed to show intentional discrimination." Based on the 1991 Act's structure and legislative history, the court determined, specifically, that a defendant must be shown to have engaged in some "egregious" misconduct before the jury is permitted to consider a request for punitive damages. Although the court declined to set out the "egregiousness" requirement in any detail, it concluded that petitioner failed to make the requisite showing in the instant case. * * *

We granted certiorari to resolve a conflict among the Federal Courts of Appeals concerning the circumstances under which a jury may consider a request for punitive damages under § 1981a(b)(1).

II

A

Prior to 1991, only equitable relief, primarily backpay, was available to prevailing Title VII plaintiffs; the statute provided no authority for an award of punitive or compensatory damages. With the passage of the 1991 Act, Congress provided for additional remedies, including punitive damages, for certain classes of Title VII and ADA violations.

The 1991 Act limits compensatory and punitive damages awards, however, to cases of "intentional discrimination"—that is, cases that do not rely on the "disparate impact" theory of discrimination. 42 U.S.C. § 1981a(a)(1). Section 1981a(b)(1) further qualifies the availability of punitive awards:

"A complaining party may recover punitive damages under this section against a respondent (other than a government, government agency or political subdivision) if the complaining party demonstrates that the respondent engaged in a discriminatory practice or discriminatory practices with malice or with reckless indifference to the federally protected rights of an aggrieved individual."

The very structure of § 1981a suggests a congressional intent o to authorize punitive awards in only a subset of cases involving intentional discrimination. Section 1981a(a)(1) limits compensatory and punitive awards to instances of intentional discrimination, while § 1981a(b)(1) requires plaintiffs to make an additional "demonstrat[ion]" of their eligibility for punitive damages. Congress plainly sought to impose two standards of liability—one for establishing a right to compensatory damages and another, higher standard that a plaintiff must satisfy to qualify for a punitive award.

The Court of Appeals sought to give life to this two-tiered structure by limiting punitive awards to cases involving intentional discrimination of an "egregious" nature. We credit the en banc majority's effort to effectuate congressional intent, but, in the end, we reject its conclusion that eligibility for punitive damages can only be described in terms of an employer's "egregious" misconduct. The terms "malice" and "reckless" ultimately focus on the actor's state of mind. While egregious misconduct is evidence of the requisite mental state, § 1981a does not limit plaintiffs to this form of evidence, and the section does not require a showing of egregious or outrageous discrimination independent of the employer's state of mind. Nor does the statute's structure imply an independent role for "egregiousness" in the face of congressional silence. On the contrary, the view that § 1981a provides for punitive awards based solely on an employer's state of mind is consistent with the 1991 Act's distinction between equitable and compensatory relief. Intent determines which remedies are open to a plaintiff here as well; compensatory awards are available only where the employer has engaged in "intentional discrimination."

Moreover, § 1981a's focus on the employer's state of mind gives some effect to Congress' apparent intent to narrow the class of cases for which punitive awards are available to a subset of those involving intentional discrimination. The employer must act with "malice or with reckless indifference to [the plaintiff's] federally protected rights." The terms "malice" or "reckless indifference" pertain to the employer's knowledge that it may be acting in violation of federal law, not its awareness that it is engaging in discrimination.

We gain an understanding of the meaning of the terms "malice" and "reckless indifference," as used in § 1981a, from this Court's decision in Smith v. Wade, 461 U.S. 30, 103 S.Ct. 1625, 75 L.Ed.2d 632 (1983). The parties, as well as both the en banc majority and dissent, recognize that Congress looked to the Court's decision in Smith in adopting this language in § 1981a. Employing language similar to what later appeared in § 1981a, the Court concluded in Smith that "a jury may be permitted to assess punitive damages in an action under § 1983 when the defendant's conduct is shown to be motivated by evil motive or intent, or when it involves reckless or callous indifference to the federally protected rights of others." While the Smith Court determined that it was unnecessary to show actual malice to qualify for a punitive award, its intent standard, at a minimum, required recklessness in its subjective form. The Court referred to a "subjective consciousness" of a risk of injury or illegality and a " 'criminal indifference to civil obligations.' " The Court thus compared the recklessness standard to the requirement that defendants act with " 'knowledge of falsity or reckless disregard for the truth' " before punitive awards are available in defamation actions. Applying this standard in the context of § 1981a, an employer must at least discriminate in the face of a perceived risk that its actions will violate federal law to be liable in punitive damages.

There will be circumstances where intentional discrimination does not give rise to punitive damages liability under this standard. In some instances, the employer may simply be unaware of the relevant federal prohibition. There will be cases, moreover, in which the employer discriminates with the distinct belief that its discrimination is lawful. The underlying theory of discrimination may be novel or otherwise poorly recognized, or an employer may reasonably believe that its discrimination satisfies a bona fide occupational qualification defense or other statutory exception to liability. In Hazen Paper Co. v. Biggins, 507 U.S. 604, 616, 113 S.Ct. 1701, 123 L.Ed.2d 338 (1993), we thus observed that, in light of statutory defenses and other exceptions permitting age-based decisionmaking, an employer may knowingly rely on age to make employment decisions without recklessly violating the Age Discrimination in Employment Act of 1967 (ADEA). Accordingly, we determined that limiting liquidated damages under the ADEA to cases where the employer "knew or showed reckless disregard for the matter of whether its conduct was prohibited by the statute," without an additional showing of outrageous conduct, was sufficient to give effect to the ADEA's two-tiered liability scheme. * * *

Egregious misconduct is often associated with the award of punitive damages, but the reprehensible character of the conduct is not generally considered apart from the requisite state of mind. Conduct warranting punitive awards has been characterized as "egregious," for example, because of the defendant's mental state. * * * That conduct committed with the specified mental state may be characterized as egregious, however, is not to say that employers must engage in conduct with some independent, "egregious" quality before being subject to a punitive award.

To be sure, egregious or outrageous acts may serve as evidence supporting an inference of the requisite "evil motive." "The allowance of exemplary damages depends upon the bad motive of the wrong-doer as exhibited by his acts." Likewise, under § 1981a(b)(1), pointing to evidence of an employer's egregious behavior would provide one means of satisfying the plaintiff's burden to "demonstrat[e]" that the employer acted with the requisite "malice or ... reckless indifference." Again, however, respondent has not shown that the terms "reckless indifference" and "malice," in the punitive damages context, have taken on a consistent definition including an independent, "egregiousness" requirement.

B

The inquiry does not end with a showing of the requisite "malice or ... reckless indifference" on the part of certain individuals, however. The plaintiff must impute liability for punitive damages to respondent. The en banc dissent recognized that agency principles place limits on vicarious liability for punitive damages. * * *

Justice STEVENS urges that we should not consider these limitations here. While we decline to engage in any definitive application of the agency standards to the facts of this case, it is important that we address the proper legal standards for imputing liability to an employer in the punitive damages context. This issue is intimately bound up with the preceding discussion on the evidentiary showing necessary to qualify for a punitive award, and it is easily subsumed within the question on which we granted certiorari—namely, "[i]n what circumstances may punitive damages be awarded under Title VII of the 1964 Civil Rights Act, as amended, for unlawful intentional discrimination?" * * *

The common law has long recognized that agency principles limit vicarious liability for punitive awards. This is a principle, moreover, that this Court historically has endorsed.

We have observed that, "[i]n express terms, Congress has directed federal courts to interpret Title VII based on agency principles." * * *

The Restatement of Agency places strict limits on the extent to which an agent's misconduct may be imputed to the principal for purposes of awarding punitive damages:

> "Punitive damages can properly be awarded against a master or other principal because of an act by an agent if, but only if:
>
> "(a) the principal authorized the doing and the manner of the act, or
>
> "(b) the agent was unfit and the principal was reckless in employing him, or
>
> "(c) the agent was employed in a managerial capacity and was acting in the scope of employment, or
>
> "(d) the principal or a managerial agent of the principal ratified or approved the act." Restatement (Second) of Agency, supra, § 217 C.

The Restatement, for example, provides that the principal may be liable for punitive damages if it authorizes or ratifies the agent's tortious act, or if it acts recklessly in employing the malfeasing agent. The Restatement also contemplates liability for punitive awards where an employee serving in a "managerial capacity" committed the wrong while "acting in the scope of employment." * * * "In making this determination, the court should review the type of authority that the employer has given to the employee, the amount of discretion that the employee has in what is done and how it is accomplished." Suffice it to say here that the examples provided in the Restatement of Torts suggest that an employee must be "important," but perhaps need not be the employer's "top management, officers, or directors," to be acting "in a managerial capacity."

Additional questions arise from the meaning of the "scope of employment" requirement. The Restatement of Agency provides that even intentional torts are within the scope of an agent's employment if the conduct is "the kind [the employee] is employed to perform," "occurs substantially within the authorized time and space limits," and "is actuated, at least in part, by a purpose to serve the" employer. Restatement (Second) of Agency, supra, § 228(1), at 504. According to the Restatement, so long as these rules are satisfied, an employee may be said to act within the scope of employment even if the employee engages in acts "specifically forbidden" by the employer and uses "forbidden means of accomplishing results." On this view, even an employer who makes every effort to comply with Title VII would be held liable for the discriminatory acts of agents acting in a "managerial capacity."

Holding employers liable for punitive damages when they engage in good faith efforts to comply with Title VII, however, is in some tension with the very principles underlying common law limitations on vicarious liability for punitive damages—that it is "improper ordinarily to award punitive damages against one who himself is personally innocent and therefore liable only vicariously." Where an employer has undertaken such good faith efforts at Title VII compliance, it "demonstrat[es] that it never acted in reckless disregard of federally protected rights."

Applying the Restatement of Agency's "scope of employment" rule in the Title VII punitive damages context, moreover, would reduce the incentive for employers to implement antidiscrimination programs. In fact, such a rule would likely exacerbate concerns among employers that § 1981a's "malice" and "reckless indifference" standard penalizes those employers who educate themselves and their employees on Title VII's prohibitions. Dissuading employers from implementing programs or policies to prevent discrimination in the workplace is directly contrary to the purposes underlying Title VII. The statute's "primary objective" is "a prophylactic one," With regard to sexual harassment, "[f]or example, Title VII is designed to encourage the creation of antiharassment policies and effective grievance mechanisms." The purposes underlying Title VII are similarly advanced where employers are encouraged to adopt antidiscrimination policies and to educate their personnel on Title VII's prohibitions.

In light of the perverse incentives that the Restatement's "scope of employment" rules create, we are compelled to modify these principles to avoid undermining the objectives underlying Title VII. Recognizing Title VII as an effort to promote prevention as well as remediation, and observing the very principles underlying the Restatements' strict limits on vicarious liability for punitive damages, we agree that, in the punitive damages context, an employer may not be vicariously liable for the discriminatory employment decisions of managerial agents where these decisions are contrary to the employer's "good-faith efforts to comply with Title VII."

We have concluded that an employer's conduct need not be independently "egregious" to satisfy § 1981a's requirements for a punitive damages award, although evidence of egregious misconduct may be used to meet the plaintiff's burden of proof. We leave for remand the question whether petitioner can identify facts sufficient to support an inference that the requisite mental state can be imputed to respondent. The parties have not yet had an opportunity to marshal the record evidence in support of their views on the application of agency principles in the instant case, and the en banc majority had no reason to resolve the issue because it concluded that petitioner had failed to demonstrate the requisite "egregious" misconduct. Although trial testimony established that Allen made the ultimate decision to promote Spangler while serving as petitioner's interim executive director, respondent's highest position, it remains to be seen whether petitioner can make a sufficient showing that Allen acted with malice or reckless indifference to petitioner's Title VII rights. Even if it could be established that Wheat effectively selected O'Donnell's replacement, moreover, several questions would remain, e.g., whether Wheat was serving in a "managerial capacity" and whether he behaved with malice or reckless indifference to petitioner's rights. It may also be necessary to determine whether the Association had been making good faith efforts to enforce an antidiscrimination policy. We leave these issues for resolution on remand.

For the foregoing reasons, the decision of the Court of Appeals is vacated, and the case is remanded for proceedings consistent with this opinion.

It is so ordered.

CHIEF JUSTICE REHNQUIST, with whom JUSTICE THOMAS joins, concurring in part and dissenting in part.

For the reasons stated by Judge Randolph in his concurring opinion in the Court of Appeals, I would hold that Congress' two-tiered scheme of Title VII monetary liability implies that there is an egregiousness requirement that reserves punitive damages only for the worst cases of intentional discrimination. Since the Court has determined otherwise, however, I join that portion of Part II–B of the Court's opinion holding that principles of agency law place a significant limitation, and in many foreseeable cases a complete bar, on employer liability for punitive damages.

JUSTICE STEVENS, with whom JUSTICE SOUTER, JUSTICE GINSBURG, and JUSTICE BREYER join, concurring in part and dissenting in part.

The Court properly rejects the Court of Appeals' holding that defendants in Title VII actions must engage in "egregious" misconduct before a jury may be permitted to consider a request for punitive damages. Accordingly, I join Parts I and II–A of its opinion. I write separately, however, because I strongly disagree with the Court's decision to volunteer commentary on an issue that the parties have not briefed and that the facts of this case do not present. I would simply remand for a trial on punitive damages.

II

In Part II–B of its opinion, the Court discusses the question "whether liability for punitive damages may be imputed to respondent" under "agency principles." That is a question that neither of the parties has ever addressed in this litigation and that respondent, at least, has expressly disavowed. When prodded at oral argument, counsel for respondent twice stood firm on this point. "[W]e all agree," he twice repeated, "that that precise issue is not before the Court" Nor did any of the 11 judges in the Court of Appeals believe that it was applicable to the dispute at hand—presumably because promotion decisions are quintessential "company acts," and because the two executives who made this promotion decision were the executive director of the Association and the acting head of its Washington office.

The absence of briefing or meaningful argument by the parties makes this Court's gratuitous decision to volunteer an opinion on this nonissue particularly ill advised. It is not this Court's practice to consider arguments—specifically, alternative defenses of the judgment under review—that were not presented in the brief in opposition to the petition for certiorari. * * *

Accordingly, while I agree with the Court's rejection of the en banc majority's holding on the only issue that it confronted, I respectfully dissent from the Court's failure to order a remand for trial on the punitive damages issue.

Page 759: New Note

The statutory authority for the EEOC to require *Federal* employers to pay compensatory damages when they intentionally discriminate in violation of Title VII is ambiguous. Only reinstatement (or hiring) with back pay is clearly authorized, However, based on the broad statutory authority to enforce the provisions of the Act "through appropriate remedies" the Court concluded that, in addition to back pay, the EEOC can order federal agencies to pay compensatory damages. *West, Secretary of Veterans Affairs v. Gibson,* ___ U.S. ___, 119 S.Ct. 1906, ___ L.Ed.2d ___ (1999).

*

STATUTORY SUPPLEMENT

Table of Contents

CIVIL RIGHTS ACT OF 1964, AS AMENDED

78 Stat. 253 (1964), as amended 86 Stat. 103 (1972),
92 Stat. 2076 (1978), 105 Stat. 1071 (1991), 109 Stat. 3 (1995)

Title VII—Equal Employment Opportunity

[Title VII, §§ 701 to 718, are classified to Subchapter VI of chapter 21 of Title 42, U.S.C.A., §§ 2000e to 2000e–17. For purposes of codification, the word "subchapter" has been substituted for "title" wherever appearing in such sections. Original section numbers are in parentheses.]

§ 2000e.   Definitions (§ 701)

For the purposes of this subchapter—

(a) The term "person" includes one or more individuals, governments, governmental agencies, political subdivisions, labor unions, partnerships, associations, corporations, legal representatives, mutual companies, joint-stock companies, trusts, unincorporated organizations, trustees, trustees in bankruptcy, or receivers.

(b) The term "employer" means a person engaged in an industry affecting commerce who has fifteen or more employees for each working day in each of twenty or more calendar weeks in the current or preceding calendar year, and any agent of such a person, but such term does not include (1) the United States, a corporation wholly owned by the Government of the United States, an Indian tribe, or any department or agency of the District of Columbia subject by statute to procedures of the competitive service (as defined in section 2102 of title 5 of the United States Code), or (2) a bona fide private membership club (other than a labor organization) which is exempt from taxation under section 501 (c) of the Internal Revenue Code of 1954[.] * * *

(c) The term "employment agency" means any person regularly undertaking with or without compensation to procure employees for an employer or to procure for employees opportunities to work for an employer and includes an agent of such a person.

(d) The term "labor organization" means a labor organization engaged in an industry affecting commerce, and any agent of such an organization, and includes any organization of any kind, any agency, or employee representation committee, group, association, or plan so engaged in which employees participate and which exists for the purpose, in whole or in part, of dealing with employers concerning grievances, labor disputes, wages, rates of pay, hours, or other terms or conditions of employment, and any conference, general committee, joint or system board, or joint council so engaged which is subordinate to a national or international labor organization.

(e) A labor organization shall be deemed to be engaged in an industry affecting commerce if (1) it maintains or operates a hiring hall or hiring office which procures employees for an employer or procures for employees opportunities to work for an employer, or (2) the number of its members (or, where it is a labor organization composed of other labor organizations or their representatives, if the aggregate number of the members of such other labor organization) is (A) twenty-five or more during the first year after the date of enactment of the Equal Employment Opportunity Act of 1972, or (B) fifteen or more thereafter, and such labor organization—

(1) is the certified representative of employees under the provisions of the National labor Relations Act, as amended, or the Railway labor Act, as amended;

(2) although not certified, is a national or international labor organization or a local labor organization recognized or acting as the representative of employees of an employer or employers engaged in an industry affecting commerce; or

(3) has chartered a local labor organization or subsidiary body which is representing or actively seeking to represent employees of employers within the meaning of paragraph (1) or (2); or

(4) has been chartered by a labor organization representing or actively seeking to represent employees within the meaning of paragraph (1) or (2) as the local or subordinate body through which such employees may enjoy membership or become affiliated with such labor organization; or

(5) is a conference, general committee, joint or system board, or joint council subordinate to a national or international labor organization, which includes a labor organization engaged in an industry affecting commerce within the meaning of any of the preceding paragraphs of this subsection.

(f) The term "employee" means an individual employed by an employer, except that the term "employee" shall not include any person elected to public office in any State or political subdivision of any State by the qualified voters thereof, or any person chosen by such officer to be on such officer's personal staff, or an appointee on the policy making level or an immediate adviser with respect to the exercise of the constitutional or legal powers of the office. The exemption set forth in the preceding sentence shall not include employees subject to the civil service laws of a State government, governmental agency or political subdivision. With respect to employment in a foreign country, such term includes an individual who is a citizen of the United States.

(g) The term "commerce" means trade, traffic, commerce, transportation, transmission, or communication among the several States; or between a State and any place outside thereof; or within the District of Columbia, or a possession of the United States; or between points in the same State but through a point outside thereof.

(h) The term "industry affecting commerce" means any activity, business, or industry in commerce or in which a labor dispute would hinder or obstruct commerce or the free flow of commerce and includes any activity or industry "affecting commerce" within the meaning of the

Labor–Management Reporting and Disclosure Act of 1959, and further includes any governmental industry, business, or activity.

(i) The term "State" includes a State of the United States, the District of Columbia, Puerto Rico, the Virgin Islands, American Samoa, Guam, Wake Island, the Canal Zone, and Outer Continental Shelf Lands defined in the Outer Continental Shelf Lands Act.

(j) The term "religion" includes all aspects of religious observance and practice, as well as belief, unless an employer demonstrates that he is unable to reasonably accommodate to an employee's or prospective employee's religious observance or practice without undue hardship on the conduct of the employer's business.

(k) The terms "because of sex" or "on the basis of sex" include, but are not limited to, because of or on the basis of pregnancy, childbirth, or related medical conditions, and women affected by pregnancy, childbirth, or related medical conditions shall be treated the same for all employment-related purposes, including receipt of benefits under fringe benefit programs, as other persons not so affected but similar in their ability or inability to work, and nothing in section 703(h) of this title shall be interpreted to permit otherwise. This subsection shall not require an employer to pay for health insurance benefits for abortion, except where the life of the mother would be endangered if the fetus were carried to term, or except where medical complications have arisen from an abortion: Provided, That nothing herein shall preclude an employer from providing abortion benefits or otherwise affect bargaining agreements in regard to abortion.

(*l*) The term "complaining party" means the Commission, the Attorney General, or a person who may bring an action or proceeding under this title.

(m) The term "demonstrates" means meets the burden of production and persuasion.

(n) The term "respondent" means an employer, employment agency, labor organization, joint labor-management committee controlling apprenticeship or other training or retraining program, including an on-the-job training program, or Federal entity subject to section 717.

§ 2000e–1. Subchapter not applicable to employment of aliens outside State and individuals for performance of activities of religious corporations, associations, educational institutions, or societies (§ 702)

(a) This title shall not apply to an employer with respect to the employment of aliens outside any State, or to a religious corporation, association, educational institution, or society with respect to the employment of individuals of a particular religion to perform work connected with the carrying on by such corporation, association, educational institution, or society of its activities.

(b) It shall not be unlawful under section 703 or 704 for an employer (or a corporation controlled by an employer), labor organization, employment agency, or joint labor-management committee con ling apprenticeship or other training or retraining (including on-th training programs) to take any action otherwise prohibited by such section, with respect to an employee in a workplace in a foreign country if compliance with such section would cause such employer (or such corporation), such organization, such agency, or such committee to violate the law of the foreign country in which such workplace is located.

(c)(1) If an employer controls a corporation whose place of incorporation is a foreign country, any practice prohibited by section 703 or 704 engaged in by such corporation shall be presumed to be engaged in by such employer.

(2) Sections 703 and 704 shall not apply with respect to the foreign operations of an employer that is a foreign person not controlled by an American employer.

(3) For purposes of this subsection, the determination of whether an employer controls a corporation shall be based on—

(A) the interrelation of operations;

(B) the common management;

(C) the centralized control of labor relations; and

(D) the common ownership or financial control of the employer and the corporation.

§ 2000e–2. Unlawful employment practices (§ 703)

(a) Employer practices

It shall be an unlawful employment practice for an employer—

(1) to fail or refuse to hire or to discharge any individual, or otherwise to discriminate against any individual with respect to his compensation, terms, conditions, or privileges of employment, because of such individual's race, color, religion, sex, or national origin; or

(2) to limit, segregate, or classify his employees or applicants for employment in any way which would deprive or tend to deprive any individual of employment opportunities or otherwise adversely affect his status as an employee, because of such individual's race, color, religion, sex, or national origin.

(b) Employment agency practices

It shall be an unlawful employment practice for an employment agency to fail or refuse to refer for employment, or otherwise to discriminate against, any individual because of his race, color, religion, sex or national origin, or to classify or refer for employment any individual on the basis of his race, color, religion, sex, or national origin.

(c) Labor organization practices

It shall be an unlawful employment practice for a labor organization—

(1) to exclude or to expel from its membership, or otherwise to discriminate against, any individual because of his race, color, religion, sex, or national origin;

(2) to limit, segregate, or classify its membership, or applicants for membership or to classify or fail or refuse to refer for employment any individual, in any way which would deprive or tend to deprive any individual of employment opportunities, or would limit such employment opportunities or otherwise adversely affect his status as an employee or as an applicant for employment, because of such individual's race, color, religion, sex, or national origin; or

(3) to cause or attempt to cause an employer to discriminate against an individual in violation of this section.

(d) Training programs

It shall be an unlawful employment practice for any employer, labor organization, or joint labor-management committee controlling apprenticeship or other training or retraining, including on-the-job training programs to discriminate against any individual because of his race, color, religion, sex, or national origin in admission to, or employment in, any program established to provide apprenticeship or other training.

(e) Businesses or enterprises with personnel qualified on basis of religion, sex, or national origin; educational institutions with personnel of particular religion

Notwithstanding any other provision of this title, (1) it shall not be an unlawful employment practice for an employer to hire and employ employees, for an employment agency to classify, or refer for employment any individual, for a labor organization to classify its membership or to classify or refer for employment any individual, or for an employer, labor organization, or joint labor-management committee controlling apprenticeship or other training or retraining programs to admit or employ any individual in any such program, on the basis of his religion, sex, or national origin in those certain instances where religion, sex, or national origin is a bona fide occupational qualification reasonably necessary to the normal operation of that particular business or enterprise, and (2) it shall not be an unlawful employment practice for a school, college, university, or other educational institution or institution of learning to hire and employ employees of a particular religion if such school, college, university, or other educational institution or institution of learning is, in whole or in substantial part, owned, supported, controlled, or managed by a particular religion or by a particular religious corporation, association, or society, or if the curriculum of such school, college, university, or other educational institution or institution of learning is directed toward the propagation of a particular religion.

(f) Members of Communist Party or Communist-action or Communist-front organizations

As used in this title, the phrase "unlawful employment practice" shall not be deemed to include any action or measure taken by an employer, labor organization, joint labor-management committee, or employment agency with respect to an individual who is a member of the Communist Party of the United States or of any other organization required to register as a Communist-action or Communist-front organization by final order of the Subversive Activities Control Board pursuant to the Subversive Activities Control Act of 1950.

(g) National security

Notwithstanding any other provision of this title, it shall not be an unlawful employment practice for an employer to fail or refuse to hire and employ any individual for any position, for an employer to discharge any individual from any position, or for an employment agency to fail or refuse to refer any individual for employment in any position, or for a labor organization to fail or refuse to refer any individual for employment in any position, if—

(1) the occupancy of such position, or access to the premises in or upon which any part of the duties of such position is performed or is to be performed, is subject to any requirement imposed in the interest of the national security of the United States under any security program in effect pursuant to or administered under any statute of the United States or any Executive order of the President; and

(2) such individual has not fulfilled or has ceased to fulfill that requirement.

(h) Seniority or merit system; quantity or quality of production; ability tests; compensation based on sex and authorized by minimum wage provisions

Notwithstanding any other provision of this title, it shall not be an unlawful employment practice for an employer to apply different standards of compensation, or different terms, conditions, or privileges of employment pursuant to a bona fide seniority or merit system, or a system which measures earnings by quantity or quality of production or to employees who work in different locations, provided that such differences are not the result of an intention to discriminate because of race, color, religion, sex, or national origin, nor shall it be an unlawful employment practice for an employer to give and to act upon the results of any professionally developed ability test provided that such test, its administration or action upon the results is not designed, intended or used to discriminate because of race, color, religion, sex or national origin. It shall not be an unlawful employment practice under this title for any employer to differentiate upon the basis of sex in determining the amount of the wages or compensation paid or to be paid to employees of such employer if such differentiation is authorized by the provisions of section 6(d) of the Fair Labor Standards Act of 1938, as amended (29 U.S.C. 206(d)).

(i) Businesses or enterprises extending preferential treatment to Indians

Nothing contained in this title shall apply to any business or enterprise on or near an Indian reservation with respect to any publicly announced employment practice of such business or enterprise under which a preferential treatment is given to any individual because he is an Indian living on or near a reservation.

(j) Preferential treatment not to be granted on account of existing number or percentage imbalance

Nothing contained in this title shall be interpreted to require any employer, employment agency, labor organization, or joint labor-management committee subject to this title to grant preferential treatment to any individual or to any group because of the race, color, religion, sex, or national origin of such individual or group on account of an imbalance which may exist with respect to the total number or percentage of persons of any race, color, religion, sex, or national origin employed by any employer, referred or classified for employment by any employment agency or labor organization, admitted to membership or classified by any labor organization, or admitted to, or employed in, any apprenticeship or other training program, in comparison with the total number or percentage of persons of such race, color, religion, sex, or national origin in any community, State, section, or other area, or in the available work force in any community, State, section, or other area.

(k) Burden of proof in disparate impact cases

(1)(A) An unlawful employment practice based on disparate impact is established under this title only if—

> (i) a complaining party demonstrates that a respondent uses a particular employment practice that causes a disparate impact on the basis of race, color, religion, sex, or national origin and the respondent fails to demonstrate that the challenged practice is job related for the position in and consistent with business necessity; or

> (ii) the complaining party makes the demonstration described in subparagraph (C) with respect to an alternative employment practice and the respondent refuses to adopt such alternative employment practice.

(B)(i) With respect to demonstrating that a particular employment practice causes a disparate impact as described in subparagraph (A)(i), the complaining party shall demonstrate that each particular challenged employment practice causes a disparate impact, except that if the complaining party can demonstrate to the court that the elements of a respondent's decision making process are not capable of separation for analysis, the decision making process maybe analyzed as one employment practice.

> (ii) If the respondent demonstrates that a specific employment practice does not cause the disparate impact, the respondent shall not be required to demonstrate that such practice is required by business necessity.

(C) The demonstration referred to by subparagraph (A)(ii) shall be in accordance with law as it existed on June 4, 1989, with respect to the concept of "alternative employment practice."

(2) A demonstration that an employment practice is required by business necessity may not be used as a defense against a claim of intentional discrimination under this title.

(3) Notwithstanding any other provision of this title, a rule barring the employment of an individual who currently and knowingly uses or possesses a controlled substance, as defined in schedules I and II of section 102(6) of the Controlled Substances Act (21 U.S.C. 802(6)), other than the use or possession of a drug taken under the supervision of a licensed health care professional, or any other use or possession authorized by the Controlled Substances Act or any other provision of Federal law, shall be considered an unlawful employment practice under this title only if such rule is adopted or applied with an intent to discriminate because of race, color, religion, sex, or national origin.

(*l*) Prohibition of discriminatory use of test scores

It shall be an unlawful employment practice for a respondent, in connection with the selection or referral of applicants or candidates for employment or promotion, to adjust the scores of, use different cutoff scores for, or otherwise alter the results of, employment related tests on the basis of race, color, religion, sex, or national origin.

(m) Impermissible consideration of race, color, religion, sex, or national origin in employment practices

Except as otherwise provided in this title, an unlawful employment practice is established when the complaining party demonstrates that race, color, religion, sex, or national origin was a motivating factor for any employment practice, even though other factors also motivated the practice.

(n) Resolution of challenges to employment practices implementing litigated or consent judgments or orders

(1)(A) Notwithstanding any other provision of law, and except as provided in paragraph (2), an employment practice that implements and is within the scope of a litigated or consent judgment or order that resolves a claim of employment discrimination under the Constitution or Federal civil rights laws may not be challenged under the circumstances described in subparagraph (B).

(B) A practice described in subparagraph (A) may not be challenged in a claim under the Constitution or Federal civil rights laws—

(i) by a person who, prior to the entry of the judgment or order described in subparagraph (A), had

(I) actual notice of the proposed judgment or order sufficient to apprise such person that such judgement or order might adversely affect the interests and legal rights of such person and that an opportunity was available to present objections to such judgment or order by a future date certain; and

       (II) a reasonable opportunity to present objections to such judgment or order; or

    (ii) by a person whose interests were adequately represented by another person who had previously challenged the judgment or order on the same legal grounds and with a similar factual situation, unless there has been an intervening change in law or fact.

(2) Nothing in this subsection shall be construed to—

    (A) alter the standards for intervention under rule 24 of the Federal Rules of Civil Procedure or apply to the rights of parties who have successfully intervened pursuant to such rule in the proceeding in which the parties intervened;

    (B) apply to the rights of parties to the action in which a litigated or consent judgment or order was entered, or of members of a class represented or sought to be represented in such action, or of members of a group on whose behalf relief was sought in such action by the Federal Government;

    (C) prevent challenges to a litigated or consent judgment or order on the ground that such judgment or order was obtained through collusion or fraud, or is transparently invalid or was entered by a court lacking subject matter jurisdiction; or

    (D) authorize or permit the denial to any person of the due process of law required by the Constitution.

(3) Any action not precluded under this subsection that challenges an employment consent judgment or order described in paragraph (1) shall be brought in the court, and if possible before the judge, that entered such judgment or order. Nothing in this subsection shall preclude a transfer of such action pursuant to section 1404 of title 28, United States Code.

§ 2000e–43. Other unlawful employment practices (§ 704)

(a) Discrimination for making charges, testifying, assisting, or participating in enforcement proceedings

It shall be an unlawful employment practice for an employer to discriminate against any of his employees or applicants for employment, for an employment agency, or joint labor-management committee controlling apprenticeship or other training or retraining, including on-the-job training programs, to discriminate against any individual, or for a labor organization to discriminate against any member thereof or applicant for membership, because he has opposed any practice made an unlawful employment practice by this title, or because he has made a charge, testified, assisted, or participated in any manner in an investigation, proceeding, or hearing under this title.

(b) Printing or publication of notices or advertisements indicating prohibited preference, limitation, specification, or discrimination; occupational qualification exception

It shall be an unlawful employment practice for an employer, labor organization, employment agency, or joint labor-management committee controlling apprenticeship or other training or retraining, including on-the-job training programs, to print or publish or cause to be printed or published any notice or advertisement relating to employment by such an employer or membership in or any classification or referral for employment by such a labor organization, or relating to any classification or referral for employment by such an employment agency, or relating to admission to, or employment in, any program established to provide apprenticeship or other training by such a joint labor-management committee indicating any preference, limitation, specification, or discrimination, based on race, color, religion, sex, or national origin, except that such a notice or advertisement may indicate a preference, limitation, specification, or discrimination based on religion, sex, or national origin when religion, sex, or national origin is a bona fide occupational qualification for employment.

§ 2000e-4.   Equal Employment Opportunity Commission (§ 705)

(a) Creation; composition; political representation; appointment; term; vacancies; Chairman and Vice Chairman; duties of Chairman; appointment of personnel; compensation of personnel

There is hereby created a Commission to be known as the Equal Employment Opportunity Commission, which shall be composed of five members, not more than three of whom shall be members of the same political party. Members of the Commission shall be appointed by the President by and with the advice and consent of the Senate for a term of five years. Any individual chosen to fill a vacancy shall be appointed only for the unexpired term of the member whom he shall succeed, and all members of the Commission shall continue to serve until their successors are appointed and qualified, except that no such member of the Commission shall continue to serve (1) for more than sixty days when the Congress is in session unless a nomination to fill such vacancy shall have been submitted to the Senate or (2) after the adjournment sine die of the session of the Senate in which such nomination was submitted. The President shall designate one member to serve as Chairman of the Commission, and one member to serve as Vice Chairman. The Chairman shall be responsible on behalf of the Commission for the administrative operations of the Commission, and except as provided in subsection (b), shall appoint, in accordance with the provisions of title 5, United States Code, governing appointments in the competitive service, such officers, agents, attorneys, administrative law judges, and employees as he deems necessary to assist it in the performance of its functions and to fix their compensation in accordance with the provisions of chapter 51 and subchapter III of chapter 53 of title 5, United States Code, relating to classification and General Schedule pay rates: Provided, that assignment, removal, and compensation of hearing examiners shall be in accordance with sections 3105, 3344, 5362, and 7521 of title 5, United States Code.

(b) General Counsel; appointment; term; duties; representation by attorneys and Attorney General

(1) There shall be a General Counsel of the Commission appointed by the President, by and with the advice and consent of the Senate, for a term of four years. The General Counsel shall have responsibility for the conduct of litigation as provided in sections 706 and 707 of this title. The General Counsel shall have such other duties as the Commission may prescribe or as may be provided by law and shall concur with the Chairman of the Commission on the appointment and supervision of regional attorneys. The General Counsel of the Commission on the effective date of this Act shall continue in such position and perform the functions specified in this subsection until a successor is appointed and qualified.

(2) Attorneys appointed under this section may, at the direction of the Commission, appear for and represent the Commission in any case in court, provided that the Attorney General shall conduct all litigation to which the Commission is a party in the Supreme Court pursuant to this title.

* * *

(g) Powers of Commission

The Commission shall have power—

(1) to cooperate with and, with their consent, utilize regional, State, local, and other agencies, both public and private, and individuals;

(2) to pay to witnesses whose depositions are taken or who are summoned before the Commission or any of its agents the same witness and mileage fees as are paid to witnesses in the courts of the United States;

(3) to furnish to persons subject to this title such technical assistance as they may request to further their compliance with this title or an order issued thereunder;

(4) upon the request of (i) any employer, whose employees or some of them, or (ii) any labor organization, whose members or some of them, refuse or threaten to refuse to cooperate in effectuating the provisions of this title, to assist in such effectuation by conciliation or such other remedial action as is provided by this title;

(5) to make such technical studies as are appropriate to effectuate the purposes and policies of this title and to make the results of such studies available to the public;

(6) to intervene in a civil action brought under section 706 by an aggrieved party against a respondent other than a government, governmental agency, or political subdivision.

* * *

§ 2000e–5. Enforcement provisions (§ 706)

(a) Power of Commission to prevent unlawful employment practices

The Commission is empowered, as hereinafter provided, to prevent any person from engaging in any unlawful employment practice as set forth in section 703 or 704 of this title.

(b) Charges by persons aggrieved or member of Commission of unlawful employment practices by employers, etc.; filing; allegations; notice to respondent; contents of notice; investigation by Commission; contents of charges; prohibition on disclosure of charges; determination of reasonable cause; conference, conciliation, and persuasion for elimination of unlawful practices; prohibition on disclosure of informal endeavors to end unlawful practices; use of evidence in subsequent proceedings; penalties for disclosure of information; time for determination of reasonable cause

Whenever a charge is filed by or on behalf of a person claiming to be aggrieved, or by a member of the Commission, alleging that an employer, employment agency, labor organization, or joint labor management committee controlling apprenticeship or other training or retraining, including on-the-job training programs, has engaged in an unlawful employment practice, the Commission shall serve a notice of the charge (including the date, place and circumstances of the alleged unlawful employment practice) on such employer, employment agency, labor organization, or joint labor-management committee (hereinafter referred to as the "respondent") within ten days, and shall make an investigation thereof. Charges shall be in writing under oath or affirmation and shall contain such information and be in such form as the Commission requires. Charges shall not be made public by the Commission. If the Commission determines after such investigation that there is not reasonable cause to believe that the charge is true, it shall dismiss the charge and promptly notify the person claiming to be aggrieved and the respondent of its action. In determining whether reasonable cause exists, the Commission shall accord substantial weight to final findings and orders made by State or local authorities in proceedings commenced under State or local law pursuant to the requirements of subsections (c) and (d). If the Commission determines after such investigation that there is reasonable cause to believe that the charge is true, the Commission shall endeavor to eliminate any such alleged unlawful employment practice by informal methods of conference, conciliation, and persuasion. Nothing said or done during and as a part of such informal endeavors may be made public by the Commission, its officers or employees, or used as evidence in a subsequent proceeding without the written consent of the cons concerned. Any person who makes public information in violation of this subsection shall be fined not more than $1,000 or imprisoned for not more than one year, or both. The Commission shall make its determination on reasonable cause as promptly as possible and, so far as practicable, not later than one hundred and twenty days from the filing of the charge or, where applicable under subsection (c) or (d) from the date upon which the Commission is authorized to take action with respect to the charge.

(c) State or local enforcement proceedings; notification of State or local authority; time for filing charges with Commission; commencement of proceedings

In the case of an alleged unlawful employment practice occurring in a State, or political subdivision of a State, which has a State or local law prohibiting the unlawful employment practice alleged and establishing or authorizing a State or local authority to grant or seek relief from such practice or to institute criminal proceedings with respect thereto upon receiving notice thereof, no charge may be filed under subsection (a) by the person aggrieved before the expiration of sixty days after proceedings have been commenced under the State or local law, unless such proceedings have been earlier terminated, provided that such sixty day period shall be extended to one hundred and twenty days during the first year after the effective date of such State or local law. If any requirement for the commencement of such proceedings is imposed by a State or local authority other than a requirement of the filing of a written and signed statement of the facts upon which the proceeding is based, the proceeding shall be deemed to have been commenced for the purposes of this subsection at the time such statement is sent by registered mail to the appropriate State or local authority.

(d) State or local enforcement proceedings; notification of State or local authority; time for action on charges by Commission

In the case of any charge filed by a member of the Commission alleging an unlawful employment practice occurring in a State or political subdivision of a State which has a State or local law prohibiting the practice alleged and establishing or authorizing a State or local authority to grant or seek relief from such practice or to institute criminal proceedings with respect thereto upon receiving notice thereof, the Commission shall, before taking any action with respect to such charge, notify the appropriate State or local officials and, upon request, afford them a reasonable time, but not less than sixty days (provided that such sixty-day period shall be extended to one hundred and twenty days during the first year after the effective date of such State or local law), unless a shorter period is requested, to act under such State or local law to remedy the practice alleged.

(e) Time for filing charges; time for service of notice of charge on respondent; filing of charge by Commission with State or local agency

(1) A charge under this section shall be filed within one hundred and eighty days after the alleged unlawful employment practice occurred and notice of the charge (including the date, place and circumstances of the alleged unlawful employment practice) shall be served upon the person against whom such charge is made within ten days thereafter, except that in a case of an unlawful employment practice with respect to which the person aggrieved has initially instituted proceedings with a State or local agency with authority to grant or seek relief from such practice or to institute criminal proceedings with respect thereto upon receiving notice thereof, such charge shall be filed by or on behalf of the person aggrieved within three hundred days after the alleged unlawful employment practice occurred, or within thirty days after receiving notice that the State or local agency has terminated the proceedings under the State or local law, whichever is earlier, and a copy of such charge shall be filed by the Commission with the State or local agency.

(2) For purposes of this section, an unlawful employment practice occurs, with respect to a seniority system that has been adopted for an intentionally discriminatory purpose in violation of this title (whether or not that discriminatory purpose is apparent on the face of the seniority provision), when the seniority system is adopted, when an individual becomes subject to the seniority system, or when a person aggrieved is injured by the application of the seniority system or provision of the system.

(f) Civil action by Commission, Attorney General, or person aggrieved; preconditions; procedure; appointment of attorney; payment of fees, costs, or security; intervention; stay of Federal proceedings; action for appropriate temporary or preliminary relief pending final disposition of charge; jurisdiction and venue of United States courts; designation of judge to hear and determine case; assignment of case for hearing; expedition of case; appointment of master

(1) If within thirty days after a charge is filed with the Commission or within thirty days after expiration of any period of reference under subsection (c) or (d), the Commission has been unable to secure from the respondent a conciliation agreement acceptable to the Commission, the Commission may bring a civil action against any respondent not a government, governmental agency, or political subdivision named in the charge. In the case of a respondent which is a government, governmental agency, or political subdivision, if the Commission has been unable to secure from the respondent a conciliation agreement acceptable to the Commission, the Commission shall take no further action and shall refer the case to the Attorney General who may bring a civil action against such respondent in the appropriate United States district court. The person or persons aggrieved shall have the right to intervene in a civil action brought by the Commission or the Attorney General in a case involving a government, governmental agency, or political subdivision. If a charge filed with the Commission pursuant to subsection is dismissed by the Commission, or if within one hundred and eighty days

from the filing of such charge or the expiration of any period of reference under subsection (c) or (d), whichever is later, the Commission has not filed a civil action under this section or the Attorney General has not filed a civil action in a case involving a government, governmental agency, or political subdivision or the Commission has not entered into a conciliation agreement to which the person aggrieved is a party, the Commission, or the Attorney General in a case involving a government, governmental agency, or political subdivision, shall so notify the person aggrieved and within ninety days after the giving of such notice a civil action may be brought against the respondent named in the charge (A) by the person claiming to be aggrieved, or (B) if such charge was filed by a member of the Commission, by any person whom the charge alleges was aggrieved by the alleged unlawful employment practice. Upon application by the complainant and in such circumstances as the court may deem just, the court may appoint an attorney for such complainant and may authorize the commencement of the action without the payment of fees, costs, or security. Upon timely application, the court may, in its discretion, permit the Commission, or the Attorney General in a case involving a government, governmental agency, or political subdivision, to intervene in such civil action upon certification that the case is of general public importance. Upon request, the court may, in its discretion, stay further proceedings for not more than sixty days pending the termination of State or local proceedings described in subsections (c) or (d) of this section or further efforts of the Commission to obtain voluntary compliance.

(2) Whenever a charge is filed with the Commission and the Commission concludes on the basis of a preliminary investigation that prompt judicial action is necessary to carry out the purposes of this Act, the Commission, or the Attorney General in a case involving a government, governmental agency, or political subdivision may bring an action for appropriate temporary or preliminary relief pending final disposition of such charge. Any temporary restraining order or other order granting preliminary or temporary relief shall be issued in accordance with rule 65 of the Federal Rules of Civil Procedure. It shall be the duty of a court having jurisdiction over proceedings under this section to assign cases for hearing at the earliest practicable date and to cause such cases to be in every way expedited.

(3) Each United States district court and each United States court of a place subject to the jurisdiction of the United States shall have jurisdiction of actions brought under this title. Such an action may be brought in any judicial district in the State in which the unlawful employment practice is alleged to have been committed, in the judicial district in which the employment records relevant to such practice are maintained and administered, or in the judicial district in which the aggrieved person would have worked but for the alleged unlawful employment practice, but if the respondent is not found within any such district, such an action may be brought within the judicial district in which the respondent has his principal office. For purposes of sections

1404 and 1406 of title 28 of the United States Code, the judicial district in which the respondent has his principal office shall in all cases be considered a district in which the action might have been brought.

(4) It shall be the duty of the chief judge of the district (or in his absence, the acting chief judge) in which the case is pending immediately to designate a judge in such district to hear and determine the case. In the event that no judge in the district is available to hear and determine the case, the chief judge of the district, or the acting chief judge, as the case may be, shall certify this fact to the chief judge of the circuit (or in his absence, the acting chief judge) who shall then designate a district or circuit judge of the circuit to hear and determine the case.

(5) It shall be the duty of the judge designated pursuant to this subsection to assign the case for hearing at the earliest practicable date and to cause the case to be in every way expedited. If such judge has not scheduled the case for trial within one hundred and twenty days after issue has been joined, that judge may appoint a master pursuant to rule 53 of the Federal Rules of Civil Procedure.

(g) Injunctions; appropriate affirmative action; equitable relief; accrual of back pay; reduction of back pay; limitations on judicial orders

(1) If the court finds that the respondent has intentionally engaged in or is intentionally engaging in an unlawful employment practice charged in the complaint, the court may enjoin the respondent from engaging in such unlawful employment practice, and order such affirmative action as may be appropriate, which may include, but is not limited to, reinstatement or hiring of employees, with or without back pay (payable by the employer, employment agency, or labor organization, as the case may be, responsible for the unlawful employment practice), or any other suitable relief as the court deems appropriate. Back pay liability shall not accrue from a date more than two years prior to the filing of a charge with the Commission. Interim earnings or amounts earnable with reasonable diligence by the person or persons discriminated against shall operate to reduce the back pay otherwise allowable.

(2)(A) No order of the court shall require the admission or reinstatement of an individual as a member of a union, or the hiring, reinstatement, or promotion of an individual as an employee, or the payment to him of any back pay, if such individual was refused admission, suspended, or expelled, or was refused employment or advancement or was suspended or discharged for any reason other than discrimination on account of race, color, religion, sex, or national origin or in violation of section 704(a).

(B) On a claim in which an individual proves a violation under section 703(m) and a respondent demonstrates that the respondent would have taken the same action in the absence of the impermissible motivating factor, the court—

(i) may grant declaratory relief, injunctive relief (except as provided in clause (ii)), and attorney's fees and costs demonstrated to be directly attributable only to the pursuit of a claim under section 703(m); and

(ii) shall not award damages or issue an order requiring any admission, reinstatement, hiring, promotion, or payment, described in subparagraph (A).

* * *

(k) Attorney's fee; liability of Commission and United States for costs

In any action or proceeding under this title the court, in its discretion, may allow the prevailing party, other than the Commission or the United States, a reasonable attorney's fee (including expert fees) as part of the costs, and the Commission and the United States shall be liable for costs the same as a private person.

§ 2000e–6.   Civil actions by the Attorney General (§ 707)

(a) Complaint

Whenever the Attorney General has reasonable cause to believe that any person or group of persons is engaged in a pattern or practice of resistance to the full enjoyment of any of the rights secured by this title, and that the pattern or practice is of such a nature and is intended to deny the full exercise of the rights herein described, the Attorney General may bring a civil action in the appropriate district court of the United States by filing with it a complaint (1) signed by him (or in his absence the Acting Attorney General), (2) setting forth facts pertaining to such pattern or practice, and (3) requesting such relief, including an application for a permanent or temporary injunction, restraining order or other order against the person or persons responsible for such pattern or practice, as he deems necessary to insure the full enjoyment of the rights herein described.

* * *

(c) Transfer of functions, etc., to Commission; effective date; prerequisite to transfer; execution of functions by Commission

Effective two years after the date of enactment of the Equal Employment Opportunity Act of 1972, the functions of the Attorney General under this section shall be transferred to the Commission[.]

* * *

(e) Investigation and action by Commission pursuant to filing of charge of discrimination; procedure

Subsequent to the date of enactment of the Equal Employment Opportunity Act of 1972, the Commission shall have authority to investigate and act on a charge of a pattern or practice of discrimination, whether filed by or on behalf of a person claiming to be aggrieved or by a member of the Commission. All such actions shall be conducted in accordance with the procedures set forth in section 706 of this Act.

§ 2000e–7. Effect on State laws (§ 708)

Nothing in this title shall be deemed to exempt or relieve any person from any liability, duty, penalty, or punishment provided by any present or future law of any State or political subdivision of a State, other than any such law which purports to require or permit the doing of any act which would be an unlawful employment practice under this title.

§ 2000e–8. Investigations (§ 709)

(a) Examination and copying of evidence related to unlawful employment practices

In connection with any investigation of a charge filed under section 706, the Commission or its designated representative shall at all reasonable times have access to, for the purposes of examination, and the right to copy any evidence of any person being investigated or proceeded against that relates to unlawful employment practices covered by this title and is relevant to the charge under investigation.

(b) Cooperation with State and local agencies administering State fair employment practices laws; participation in and contribution to research and other projects; utilization of services; payment in advance or reimbursement; agreements and rescission of agreements

The Commission may cooperate with State and local agencies charged with the administration of State fair employment practices laws and, with the consent of such agencies, may, for the purpose of carrying out its functions and duties under this title and within the limitation of funds appropriated specifically for such purpose, engage in and contribute to the cost of research and other projects of mutual interest undertaken by such agencies, and utilize the services of such agencies and their employees, and, notwithstanding any other provision of law, advance or reimbursement such agencies and their employees for services rendered to assist the Commission in carrying out this title. In furtherance of such cooperative efforts, the Commission may enter into written agreements with such State or local agencies and such agreements may include provisions under which the Commission shall refrain from processing a charge in any cases or class of cases specified in such agreements or under which the Commission shall relieve any person or class of persons in such State or locality from requirements imposed under this section. The Commission shall rescind any such agreement whenever it determines that the agreement no longer serves the interest of effective enforcement of this title.

(c) Execution, retention, and preservation of records; reports to Commission; training program records; appropriate relief from regulation or order for undue hardship; procedure for exemption; judicial action to compel compliance

Every employer, employment agency, and labor organization subject to this title shall (1) make and keep such records relevant to the determinations of whether unlawful employment practices have been or are being committed, (2) preserve such records for such periods, and (3) make such reports therefrom, as the Commission shall prescribe by regulation or order, after public hearing, as reasonable, necessary, or appropriate for the enforcement of this title or the regulations or orders thereunder. The Commission shall, by regulation, require each employer, labor organization, and joint labor-management committee subject to this title which controls an apprenticeship or other training program to maintain such records as are reasonably necessary to carry out the purpose of this title, including, but not limited to, a list of applicants who wish to participate in such program, including the chronological order in which applications were received, and to furnish to the Commission upon request, a detailed description of the manner in which persons are selected to participate in the apprenticeship or other training program. Any employer, employment agency, labor organization, or joint labor-management committee which believes that the application to it of any regulation or order issued under this section would result in undue hardship may apply to the Commission for an exemption from the application of such regulation or order, and, if such application for an exemption is denied, bring a civil action in the United States district court for the district where such records are kept. If the Commission or the court, as the case may be, finds that the application of the regulation or order to the employer, employment agency, or labor organization in question would impose an undue hardship, the Commission or the court, as the case may be, may grant appropriate relief. If any person required to comply with the provisions of this subsection fails or refuses to do so, the United States district court for the district in which such person is found, resides, or transacts business, shall, upon application of the Commission, or the Attorney General in a case involving a government, governmental agency or political subdivision, have jurisdiction to issue to such person an order requiring him to comply.

* * *

For the purpose of all hearings and investigations conducted by the Commission or its duly authorized agents or agencies, section 11 of the National labor Relations Act (49 Stat. 455: 29 U.S.C. 161) shall apply.

§ 2000e–10. Posting of notices; penalties (§ 711)

(a) Every employer, employment agency, and labor organization, as the case may be, shall post and keep posted in conspicuous places upon its premises where notices to employees, applicants for employment, and members are customarily posted a notice to be prepared or approved by the Commission setting forth excerpts from, or summaries of, the pertinent provisions of this title and information pertinent to the filing of a complaint.

(b) A willful violation of this section shall be punishable by a fine of not more than $100 for each separate offense.

§ 2000e–11.   Veterans' special rights or preference (§ 712)

Nothing contained in this title shall be construed to repeal or modify any Federal, State, territorial, or local law creating special rights or preference for veterans.

§ 2000e–12.   Regulations; conformity of regulations with administrative procedure provisions; reliance on interpretations and instructions of Commission (§ 713)

(a) The Commission shall have authority from time to time to issue, amend, or rescind suitable procedural regulations to carry out the provisions of this title. Regulations issued under the section shall be in conformity with the standards and limitations of the Administrative Procedure Act.

* * *

§ 2000e–14.   Equal Employment Opportunity Coordinating Council; establishment; composition; duties; report to President and Congress (§ 715)

The Equal Employment Opportunity Commission shall have the responsibility for developing and implementing agreements, policies and practices designed to maximize effort, promote efficiency, and eliminate conflict, competition, duplication and inconsistency among the operations, functions and jurisdictions of the various departments, agencies and branches of the Federal government responsible for the implementation and enforcement of equal employment opportunity legislation, orders, and policies. On or before October 1 of each year, the Council shall transmit to the President and to the Congress a report of its activities, together with such recommendations for legislative or administrative changes as it concludes are desirable to further promote the purposes of this section.

§ 2000e–16.   Employment by Federal Government (§ 717)

(a) Discriminatory practices prohibited: employees or applicants for employment subject to coverage

All personnel actions affecting employees or applicants for employment (except with regard to aliens employed outside the limits of the United States) in military departments as defined in section 102 of title 5, United States Code, in executive agencies as defined in section 105 of title 5, United States Code (including employees and applicants for employment who are paid from nonappropriated funds), in the United States Postal Service and the Postal Rate Commission, in those units of the Government of the District of Columbia having positions in the competitive service, and in those units of the judicial branch of the

Federal Government having positions in the competitive service, and in the Government Printing Office, the General Accounting Office, and the Library of Congress shall be made free from any discrimination based on race, color, religion, sex, or national origin.

(b) Equal Employment Opportunity Commission; enforcement powers; issuance of rules, regulations, etc.; annual review and approval of national and regional equal employment opportunity plans; review and evaluation of equal employment opportunity programs and publication of progress reports; consultations with interested parties; compliance with rules, regulations, etc.; contents of national and regional equal employment opportunity plans; authority of Librarian of Congress

Except as otherwise provided in this subsection, the Equal Employment Opportunity Commission shall have authority to enforce the provisions of subsection (a) through appropriate remedies, including reinstatement or hiring of employees with or without back pay, as will effectuate the policies of this section, and shall issue such rules, regulations, orders, and instructions as it deems necessary and appropriate to carry out its responsibilities under this section. The Equal Employment Opportunity Commission shall—

(1) be responsible for the annual review and approval of a national and regional equal employment opportunity plan which each department and agency and each appropriate unit referred to in subsection (a) of this section shall submit in order to maintain an affirmative program of equal employment opportunity for all such employees and applicants for employment:

(2) be responsible for the review and evaluation of the operation of all agency equal employment opportunity programs, periodically obtaining and publishing (on at least a semiannual basis) progress reports from each such department, agency, or unit: and

(3) consult with and solicit the recommendations of interested individuals, groups, and organizations relating to equal employment opportunity.

The head of each such department, agency, or unit shall comply with such rules, regulations, orders, and instructions which shall include a provision that an employee or applicant for employment shall be notified of any final action taken on any complaint of discrimination filed by him thereunder. The plan submitted by each department, agency, and unit shall include, but not be limited to—

(1) provision for the establishment of training and education programs designed to provide a maximum opportunity for employees to advance so as to perform at their highest potential; and

(2) a description of the qualifications in terms of training and experience relating to equal employment opportunity for the principal and operating officials of each such department, agency, or unit responsible for carrying out the equal employment opportunity

program and of the allocation of personnel and resources proposed by such department, agency, or unit to carry out its equal employment opportunity program.

With respect to employment in the Library of Congress, authorities granted in this subsection to the Civil Service Commission shall be exercised by the Librarian of Congress.

(c) Civil action by employee or applicant for employment for redress of grievances; time for bringing of action; head of department, agency, or unit as defendant

Within ninety days of receipt of notice of final action taken by a department, agency, or unit referred to in subsection 717(a), or by the Civil Service Commission upon an appeal from a decision or order of such department, agency, or unit on a complaint of discrimination based on race, color, religion, sex, or national origin, brought pursuant to subsection (a) of this section, Executive Order I 1478 or any succeeding Executive orders, or after one hundred and eighty days from the filing of the initial charge with the department, agency, or unit or with the Civil Service Commission on appeal from a decision or order of such department, agency, or unit until such time as final action may be taken by a department, agency, or unit, an employee or applicant for employment, if aggrieved by the final disposition of his complaint, or by the failure to take final action on his complaint, may file a civil action as provided in section 706, in which civil action the head of the department, agency, or unit, as appropriate, shall be the defendant.

(d) Section 2000e–5(f) through (k) of this title applicable to civil actions

The provisions of section 706(f) through (k), as applicable, shall govern civil actions brought hereunder, and the same interest to compensate for delay in payment shall be available as in cases involving nonpublic parties.

(e) Government agency or official not relieved of responsibility to assure nondiscrimination in employment or equal employment opportunity

Nothing contained in this Act shall relieve any Government agency or official of its or his primary responsibility to assure nondiscrimination in employment as required by the Constitution and statutes or of its or his responsibilities under Executive Order 11478 relating to equal employment opportunity in the Federal Government.

§ 2000e–17.   Procedure for denial, withholding, termination, or suspension of Government contract subsequent to acceptance by Government of affirmative action plan of employer; time of acceptance of plan (§ 718)

No Government contract, or portion thereof, with any employer, shall be denied, withheld, terminated, or suspended, by any agency or officer of the United States under any equal employment opportunity law or order, where such employer has an affirmative action plan which has previously been accepted by the Government for the same facility within the past twelve months without first according such employer full hearing and adjudication under the provisions of title 5, United States Code, section 554, and the following pertinent sections: Provided, that if such employer has deviated substantially from such previously agreed to affirmative action plan, this section shall not apply: Provided further, That for the purposes of this section an affirmative action plan shall be deemed to have been accepted by the Government at the time the appropriate compliance agency has accepted such plan unless within forty-five days thereafter the Office of Federal Contract Compliance has disapproved such plan.

SECTIONS 1981 AND 1981(A)

42 U.S.C. § 1981.[1] Equal rights under the law.

(a) All persons within the jurisdiction of the United States shall have the same right in every State and Territory to make and enforce contracts, to sue, be parties, give evidence, and to the full and dual benefit of all laws and proceedings for the security of persons and property as is enjoyed by white citizens, and shall be subject to like punishment, pains, penalties, taxes, licenses, and exactions of every kind, and to no other.

(b) For purposes of this section, the term "make and enforce contracts" includes the making, performance, modification, and termination of contracts, and the enjoyment of all benefits, privileges, terms and conditions of the contractual relationship.

(c) The rights protected by this section are protected against impairment by nongovernmental discrimination and impairment under color of State law.

42 U.S.C. § 1981A.[2] "Damages in Cases of Intentional Discrimination in Employment."

(a) Right of Recovery.

(1) Civil rights.

In an action brought by a complaining party under section 706 or 717 of the Civil Rights Act of 1964 (42 U.S.C. 2000e–5) against a respondent who engaged in unlawful intentional discrimination (not an employment practice that is unlawful because of its disparate impact) prohibited under section 703, 704, or 717 of the Act (42 U.S.C. 2000e–2 or 2000e–3), and provided that the complaining party cannot recover under section 1977 of the Revised Statutes (42 U.S.C. 1981), the complaining party may recover compensatory and punitive damages as allowed in subsection (b), in addition to any relief authorized by section 706(g) of the Civil Rights Act of 1964, from the respondent.

(2) Disability

...ought by a complaining party under the powers, ...nd procedures set forth in section 706 or 717 of the Civil ...Act of 1964 (as provided in section 107(a) of the Americans ...th Disabilitie... Act of 1990 (42 U.S.C. 12117(a)), and section 505(a)(1) of the Rehabilitation Act of 1973 (29 U.S.C. 794a(a)(1)), respectively) against a respondent who engaged in unlawful intentional discrimination (not an employment practice that is unlawful because of its disparate impact) under section 501 of the Rehabi...

---

1. Derived from § 1 of the Civil Rights Act of 1866 and §§ 16 and 18 of the Civil Rights Act of 1870. 14 Stat. 27; 16 Stat. 144. In the 1874 revision of the United States Code, it was codified as § 1977. 18

Stat. 348. Amended by the C... of 1991. 105 Stat. 1071 (1...

2. Added by th... 1991. 105 Stat...

tion Act of 1973 (29 U.S.C. 791) and the regulations implementing section 501, or who violated the requirements of section 501 of the Act or the regulations implementing section 501 concerning the provisions of a reasonable accommodation, or section 102 of the Americans with Disabilities Act of 1990 (42 U.S.C. 12112), or committed a violation of section 102(b)(5) of the Act, against an individual, the complaining party may recover compensatory and punitive damages as allowed in subsection (b), in addition to any relief authorized by section 706(g) of the Civil Rights Act of 1964, from the respondent.

(3) Reasonable accommodation and good faith effort.

In cases where a discriminatory practice involves the provision of a reasonable accommodation pursuant to section 102(b)(5) of the Americans with Disabilities act of 1990 or regulations implementing section 501 of the Rehabilitation Act of 1973, damages may not be awarded under this section where the covered entity demonstrates good faith efforts, in consultation with the person with the disability who has informed the covered entity that accommodation is needed, to identify and make a reasonable accommodation that would provide such individual with an equally effective opportunity and would not cause an undue hardship on the operation of the business.

(b) Compensatory and Punitive Damages.

(1) Determination of punitive damages.

A complaining party may recover punitive damages under this section against a respondent (other than a government, government agency or political subdivision) if the complaining party demonstrates that the respondent engaged in a discriminatory practice or discriminatory practices with malice or with reckless indifference to the federally protected rights of an aggrieved individual.

(2) Exclusions from compensatory damages.

Compensatory damages awarded under this section shall not include backpay, interest on backpay, or any relief authorized under section 706(g) of the Civil Rights

(3) Limitations.

The sum of the amount of compensatory damages awarded under this section for future pecuniary losses, emotional pain, suffering, inconvenience, mental anguish, loss of enjoyment of life, and other nonpecuniary losses, and the amount of punitive damages awarded under this section, shall not exceed, for each complaining party.

(A) in the case of a respondent who has more than 14 and fewer than 101 employees in each of 20 or more calendar weeks in the current or preceding calendar year, $50,000;

(B) in the case of a respondent who has more than 100 and fewer than 201 employees in each of 20 or more calendar weeks in the current or preceding calendar year, $100,000; and

(C) in the case of a respondent who has more than 200 and fewer than 501 employees in each of 20 or more calendar weeks in the current or preceding calendar year, $200,000; and

(D) in the case of a respondent who has more than 500 employees in each of 20 or more calendar weeks in the current or preceding calendar year, $300,000.

(4) Construction.

Nothing in this section shall be construed to limit the scope of, or the relief available under, section 1977 of the Revised Statutes (42 U.S.C. 1981).

(c) Jury Trial.

If a complaining party seeks compensatory or punitive damages under this section

(1) any party may demand a trial by jury; and

(2) the court shall not inform the jury of the limitations described in subsection (b)(3).

(d) Definitions.

As used in this section:

(1) Complaining party.

The term "complaining party" means

(A) in the case of a person seeking to bring an action under subsection (a)(1), the Equal Employment Opportunity Commission, the Attorney General, or a person who may bring an action or proceeding under title VII of the Civil Rights Act of 1964 (42 U.S.C. 2000e et seq.); or

(B) in the case of a person seeking to bring an action under subsection (a)(2), the Equal Employment Opportunity Commission, the Attorney General, a person who may bring an action or proceeding under section 505(a)(1) of the Rehabilitation Act of 1973 (29 U.S.C. 794a(a)(1), or a person who may bring an action or proceeding under title I of the Americans with Disabilities Act of 1990 (42 U.S.C. 12101 et seq.).

(2) Discriminatory practice.

The term "discriminatory practice" means the discrimination described in paragraph (1), or the discrimination or the violation described in paragraph (2), of subsection (a).

AGE DISCRIMINATION IN EMPLOYMENT ACT

81 Stat. 602 (1967), as amended 92 Stat. 189 (1978)
100 Stat. 3342 (1986), 104 Stat. 978 (1990), 109 Stat. 3 (1995)

§ 621. Congressional statement of findings and purpose

(a) The Congress hereby finds and declares that—

(1) in the face of rising productivity and affluence, older workers find themselves disadvantaged in their efforts to retain employment, and especially to regain employment when displaced from jobs;

(2) the setting of arbitrary age limits regardless of potential for job performance has become a common practice, and certain otherwise desirable practices may work to the disadvantage of older persons;

(3) the incidence of unemployment, especially long-term unemployment with resultant deterioration of skill, morale, and employer acceptability is, relative to the younger ages, high among older workers; their numbers are great and growing; and their employment problems grave;

(4) the existence in industries affecting commerce, of arbitrary discrimination in employment because of age, burdens commerce and the free flow of goods in commerce.

(b) It is therefore the purpose of this chapter to promote employment of older persons based on their ability rather than age; to prohibit arbitrary age discrimination in employment; to help employers and workers find ways of meeting problems arising from the impact of age on employment.

* * *

§ 623. Prohibition of age discrimination

(a) Employer practices

It shall be unlawful for an employer—

(1) to fail or refuse to hire or to discharge any individual or otherwise discriminate against any individual with respect to his compensation, terms, conditions, or privileges of employment, because of such individual's age;

(2) to limit, segregate, or classify his employees in any way which would deprive or tend to deprive any individual of employment opportunities or otherwise adversely affect his status as an employee, because of such individual's age; or

(3) to reduce the wage rate of any employee in order to comply with this chapter.

(b) Employment agency practices

It shall be unlawful for an employment agency to fail or refuse to refer for employment, or otherwise to discriminate against, any individual because of such individual's age, or to classify or refer for employment any individual on the basis of such individual's age.

(c) Labor organization practices

It shall be unlawful for a labor organization—

(1) to exclude or to expel from its membership, or otherwise to discriminate against, any individual because of his age;

(2) to limit, segregate, or classify its membership, or to classify or fail or refuse to refer for employment any individual, in any way which would deprive or tend to deprive any individual of employment opportunities, or would limit such employment opportunities or otherwise adversely affect his status as an employee or as an applicant for employment, because of such individual's age;

(3) to cause or attempt to cause an employer to discriminate against an individual in violation of this section.

(d) Opposition to unlawful practices; participation in investigations, proceedings, or litigation

It shall be unlawful for an employer to discriminate against any of his employees or applicants for employment, for an employment agency to discriminate against any individual, or for a labor organization to discriminate against any member thereof or applicant for membership, because such individual, member or applicant for membership has opposed any practice made unlawful by this section, or because such individual, member or applicant for membership has made a charge, testified, assisted, or participated in any manner in an investigation, proceeding, or litigation under this chapter.

(e) Printing or publication of notice or advertisement indicating preference, limitation, etc.

It shall be unlawful for an employer, labor organization, or employment agency to print or publish, or cause to be printed or published, any notice or advertisement relating to employment by such an employer or membership in or any classification or referral for employment by such a labor organization, or relating to any classification or referral for employment by such an employment agency, indicating any preference, limitation, specification, or discrimination, based on age.

(f) Lawful practices; age an occupational qualification; other reasonable factors; laws of foreign workplace; seniority system; employee benefit plans; discharge or discipline for good cause

It shall not be unlawful for an employer, employment agency, or labor organization—

(1) to take any action otherwise prohibited under subsections (a), (b), (c), or (e) of this section where age is a bona fide occupational qualification reasonably necessary to the normal operation of the particular business, or where the differentiation is based on reasonable factors

other than age, or where such practices involve an employee in a workplace in a foreign country, and compliance with such subsections would cause such employer, or a corporation controlled by such employer, to violate the laws of the country in which such workplace is located;

(2) to take any action otherwise prohibited under subsection (a), (b), (c), or (e) of this section—

(A) to observe the terms of a bona fide seniority system that is not intended to evade the purposes of this chapter, except that no such seniority system shall require or permit the involuntary retirement of any individual specified by section 631(a) of this title because of the age of such individual; or

(B) to observe the terms of a bona fide employee benefit plan—

(i) where, for each benefit or benefit package, the actual amount of payment made or cost incurred on behalf of an older worker is no less than that made or incurred on behalf of a younger worker, as permissible under section 1625.10, title 29, Code of Federal Regulations (as in effect on June 22, 1989); or

(ii) that is a voluntary early retirement incentive plan consistent with the relevant purpose or purposes of this chapter.

Notwithstanding clause (i) or (ii) of subparagraph (B), no such employee benefit plan or voluntary early retirement incentive plan shall excuse the failure to hire any individual, and no such employee benefit plan shall require or permit the involuntary retirement of any individual specified by section 631(a) of this title, because of the age of such individual. An employer, employment agency, or labor organization acting under subparagraph (A), or under clause (i) or (ii) of subparagraph (B), shall have the burden of proving that such actions are lawful in any civil enforcement proceeding brought under this chapter; or

(3) to discharge or otherwise discipline an individual for good cause.

(h) Practices of foreign corporations controlled by American employers; foreign persons not controlled by American employers; factors determining control

(1) If an employer controls a corporation whose place of incorporation is in a foreign country, any practice by such corporation prohibited under this section shall be presumed to be such practice by such employer.

(2) The prohibitions of this section shall not apply where the employer is a foreign person not controlled by an American employer.

(3) For the purpose of this subsection the determination of whether an employer controls a corporation shall be based upon the—

(A) interrelation of operations,

(B) common management,

(C) centralized control of labor relations, and

(D) common ownership or financial control, of the employer and the corporation.

(i) Employee pension benefit plans; cessation or reduction of benefit accrual or of allocation to employee account; distribution of benefits after attainment of normal retirement age; compliance; highly compensated employees

(1) Except as otherwise provided in this subsection, it shall be unlawful for an employer, an employment agency, a labor organization, or any combination thereof to establish or maintain an employee pension benefit plan which requires or permits—

(A) in the case of a defined benefit plan, the cessation of an employee's benefit accrual, or the reduction of the rate of an employee's benefit accrual, because of age, or

(B) in the case of a defined contribution plan, the cessation of allocations to an employee's account, or the reduction of the rate at which amounts are allocated to an employee's account, because of age.

(2) Nothing in this section shall be construed to prohibit an employer, employment agency, or labor organization from observing any provision of an employee pension benefit plan to the extent that such provision imposes (without regard to age) a limitation on the amount of benefits that the plan provides or a limitation on the number of years of service or years of participation which are taken into account for purposes of determining benefit accrual under the plan.

(3) In the case of any employee who, as of the end of any plan year under a defined benefit plan, has attained normal retirement age under such plan—

(A) if distribution of benefits under such plan with respect to such employee has commenced as of the end of such plan year, then any requirement of this subsection for continued accrual of benefits under such plan with respect to such employee during such plan year shall be treated as satisfied to the extent of the actuarial equivalent of in-service distribution of benefits, and

(B) if distribution of benefits under such plan with respect to such employee has not commenced as of the end of such year in accordance with section 1056(a)(3) of this title and section 401(a)(14)(C) of title 26, and the payment of benefits under such plan with respect to such employee is not suspended during such plan year pursuant to section 1053(a)(3)(B) of this title or section 411(a)(3)(B) of title 26, then any requirement of this subsection for continued accrual of benefits under such plan with respect to such employee during such plan year shall be treated as satisfied to the extent of any adjustment in the benefit payable under the plan during such plan year attributable to the delay in the distribution of benefits after the attainment of normal retirement age. The provisions of this paragraph shall apply in accordance with regulations of the Secretary of the Treasury. Such regulations shall provide for the application of the preceding provisions of this paragraph to all employee pension benefit plans subject to this subsection and may provide for the application of such provisions, in the case of any such employee, with respect to any period of time within a plan year.

(4) Compliance with the requirements of this subsection with respect to an employee pension benefit plan shall constitute compliance with the requirements of this section relating to benefit accrual under such plan.

(5) Paragraph (1) shall not apply with respect to any employee who is a highly compensated employee (within the meaning of section 414(q) of title 26) to the extent provided in regulations prescribed by the Secretary of the Treasury for purposes of precluding discrimination in favor of highly compensated employees within the meaning of subchapter D of chapter 1 of title 26.

(6) A plan shall not be treated as failing to meet the requirements of paragraph (1) solely because the subsidized portion of any early retirement benefit is disregarded in determining benefit accruals.

(7) Any regulations prescribed by the Secretary of the Treasury pursuant to clause (v) of section 411(b)(1)(H) of title 26 and subparagraphs (C) and (D) of section 411(b)(2) of title 26 shall apply with respect to the requirements of this subsection in the same manner and to the same extent as such regulations apply with respect to the requirements of such sections 411(b)(1)(H) and 411(b)(2) of title 26.

(8) A plan shall not be treated as failing to meet the requirements of this section solely because such plan provides a normal retirement age described in section 1002(24)(B) of this title and section 411(a)(8)(B) of title 26.

For purposes of this subsection—

(A) The terms "employee pension benefit plan", "defined benefit plan", "defined contribution plan", and "normal retirement age" have the meanings provided such terms in section 1002 of this title.

(B) The term "compensation" has the meaning provided by section 414(s) of title 26.

(k) Date of adoption of system or plan

A seniority system or employee benefit plan shall comply with this chapter regardless of the date of adoption of such system or plan.

(*l*) Minimum age requirements; early retirement benefits

Notwithstanding clause (i) or (ii) of subsection (f)(2)(B) of this section—

(1) It shall not be a violation of subsection (a), (b), (c), or (e) of this section solely because—

(A) an employee pension benefit plan (as defined in section 1002(2) of this title) provides for the attainment of a minimum age as a condition of eligibility for normal or early retirement benefits; or

(B) a defined benefit plan (as defined in section 1002(35) of this title) provides for—

(i) payments that constitute the subsidized portion of an early retirement benefit; or

(ii) social security supplements for plan participants that commence before the age and terminate at the age (specified by the plan) when participants are eligible to receive reduced or unreduced old-age insurance benefits under title II of the Social Security Act (42 U.S.C. § 401 et seq.), and that do not exceed such old-age insurance benefits.

(2)(A) It shall not be a violation of subsection (a), (b), (c), or (e) of this section solely because following a contingent event unrelated to age—

(i) the value of any retiree health benefits received by an individual eligible for an immediate pension;

(ii) the value of any additional pension benefits that are made available solely as a result of the contingent event unrelated to age and following which the individual is eligible for not less than an immediate and unreduced pension; or

(iii) the values described in both clauses (i) and (ii);

are deducted from severance pay made available as a result of the contingent event unrelated to age.

(B) For an individual who receives immediate pension benefits that are actuarially reduced under subparagraph (A)(i), the amount of the deduction available pursuant to subparagraph (A)(i) shall be reduced by the same percentage as the reduction in the pension benefits.

(C) For purposes of this paragraph, severance pay shall include that portion of supplemental unemployment compensation benefits (as described in section 501(c)(17) of Title 26) that—

(i) constitutes additional benefits of up to 52 weeks;

(ii) has the primary purpose and effect of continuing benefits until an individual becomes eligible for an immediate and unreduced pension; and

(iii) is discontinued once the individual becomes eligible for an immediate and unreduced pension.

(D) For purposes of this paragraph and solely in order to make the deduction authorized under this paragraph, the term "retiree health benefits" means benefits provided pursuant to a group health plan covering retirees, for which (determined as of the contingent event unrelated to age)—

(i) the package of benefits provided by the employer for the retirees who are below age 65 is at least comparable to benefits provided under title XVIII of the Social Security Act (42 U.S.C. § 1395 et seq.);

(ii) the package of benefits provided by the employer for the retirees who are age 65 and above is at least comparable to that offered under a plan that provides a benefit package with one-fourth the value of benefits provided under title XVIII of such Act; or

(iii) the package of benefits provided by the employer is as described in clauses (i) and (ii).

(E)(i) If the obligation of the employer to provide retiree health benefits is of limited duration, the value for each individual shall be calculated at a rate of $3,000 per year for benefit years before age 65, and $750 per year for benefit years beginning at age 65 and above.

(ii) If the obligation of the employer to provide retiree health benefits is of unlimited duration, the value for each individual shall be calculated at a rate of $48,000 for individuals below age 65, and $24,000 for individuals age 65 and above.

(iii) The values described in clauses (i) and (ii) shall be calculated based on the age of the individual as of the date of the contingent event unrelated to age. The values are effective on October 16, 1990, and shall be adjusted on an annual basis, with respect to a contingent event that occurs subsequent to the first year after October 16, 1990, based on the medical component of the Consumer Price Index for all-urban consumers published by the Department of Labor.

(iv) If an individual is required to pay a premium for retiree health benefits, the value calculated pursuant to this subparagraph shall be reduced by whatever percentage of the overall premium the individual is required to pay.

(F) If an employer that has implemented a deduction pursuant to subparagraph (A) fails to fulfill the obligation described in subparagraph (E), any aggrieved individual may bring an action for specific performance of the obligation described in subparagraph (E). The relief shall be in addition to any other remedies provided under Federal or State law.

(3) It shall not be a violation of subsection (a), (b), (c), or (e) of this section solely because an employer provides a bona fide employee benefit plan or plans under which long-term disability benefits received by an individual are reduced by any pension benefits (other than those attributable to employee contributions)—

(A) paid to the individual that the individual voluntarily elects to receive; or

(B) for which an individual who has attained the later of age 62 or normal retirement age is eligible.

* * *

§ 625.   Administration

The Secretary * * * shall have the power—

(a) Delegation of functions; appointment of personnel; technical assistance to make delegations, to appoint such agents and employees, and to pay for technical assistance on a fee for service basis, as he deems necessary to assist him in the performance of his functions under this chapter;

(b) Cooperation with other agencies, employers, labor organizations, and employment agencies to cooperate with regional, State, local, and other agencies, and to cooperate with and furnish technical assistance to employers, labor organizations, and employment agencies to aid in effectuating the purposes of this chapter.

§ 626.   Recordkeeping, investigation, and enforcement

(a) **Attendance of witnesses; investigations, inspections, records, and homework regulations**

The Equal Employment Opportunity Commission shall have the power to make investigations and require the keeping of records necessary or appropriate for the administration of this chapter in accordance with the powers and procedures provided in sections 209 and 211 of this title.

(b) **Enforcement; prohibition of age discrimination under fair labor standards; unpaid minimum wages and unpaid overtime compensation; liquidated damages; judicial relief; conciliation, conference, and persuasion**

The provisions of this chapter shall be enforced in accordance with the powers, remedies, and procedures provided in sections 211(b), 216 (except for subsection (a) thereof), and 217 of this title, and subsection (c) of this section. Any act prohibited under section 623 of this title shall be deemed to be a prohibited act under section 215 of this title. Amounts owing to a person as a result of a violation of this chapter shall be deemed to be unpaid minimum wages or unpaid overtime compensation for purposes of sections 216 and 217 of this title: *Provided*, That liquidated damages shall be payable only in cases of willful violations of this chapter. In any action brought to enforce this chapter the court shall have jurisdiction to grant such legal or equitable relief as may be appropriate to effectuate the purposes of this chapter, including without limitation judgments compelling employment, reinstatement or promotion, or enforcing the liability for amounts deemed to be unpaid minimum wages or unpaid overtime compensation under this section. Before instituting any action under this section, the Equal Employment

Opportunity Commission shall attempt to eliminate the discriminatory practice or practices alleged, and to effect voluntary compliance with the requirements of this chapter through informal methods of conciliation, conference, and persuasion.

(c) Civil actions; persons aggrieved; jurisdiction; judicial relief; termination of individual action upon commencement of action by Commission; jury trial

(1) Any person aggrieved may bring a civil action in any court of competent jurisdiction for such legal or equitable relief as will effectuate the purposes of this chapter: Provided, That the right of any person to bring such action shall terminate upon the commencement of an action by the [Equal Employment Opportunity Commission] to enforce the right of such employee under this chapter.

(2) In an action brought under paragraph (1), a person shall be entitled to a trial by jury of any issue of fact in any such action for recovery of amounts owing as a result of a violation of this chapter, regardless of whether equitable relief is sought by any party in such action.

(d) Filing of charge with Commission; timeliness; conciliation, conference, and persuasion

No civil action may be commenced by an individual under this section until 60 days after a charge alleging unlawful discrimination has been filed with the Equal Employment Opportunity Commission. Such a charge shall be filed—

> (1) within 180 days after the alleged unlawful practice occurred; or

> (2) in a case to which section 633(b) of this title applies, within 300 days after the alleged unlawful practice occurred, or within 30 days after receipt by the individual of notice of termination of proceedings under State law, whichever is earlier.

Upon receiving such a charge, the Commission shall promptly notify all persons named in such charge as prospective defendants in the action and shall promptly seek to eliminate any alleged unlawful practice by informal methods of conciliation, conference, and persuasion.

(e) Statute of limitations; reliance in future on administrative ruling, etc.; tolling

(1) Sections 255 and 259 of this title shall apply to actions under this chapter.

(2) For the period during which the Equal Employment Opportunity Commission is attempting to effect voluntary compliance with requirements of this chapter through informal methods of conciliation, conference, and persuasion pursuant to subsection (b) of this section, the statute of limitations as provided in section 255 of this title shall be tolled, but in no event for a period in excess of one year.

§ 627. Notices to be posted

Every employer, employment agency, and labor organization shall post and keep posted in conspicuous places upon its premises a notice to be prepared or approved by the Equal Employment Opportunity Commission setting forth information as the Commission deems appropriate to effectuate the purposes of this chapter.

§ 628. Rules and regulations; exemptions

In accordance with the provisions of subchapter II of chapter 5 of Title 5, the Equal Employment Opportunity Commission may issue such rules and regulations as it may consider necessary or appropriate for carrying out this chapter, and may establish such reasonable exemptions to and from any or all provisions of this chapter as it may find necessary and proper in the public interest.

* * *

§ 630. Definitions

For the purposes of this chapter—

(a) The term "person" means one or more individuals, partnerships, associations, labor organizations, corporations, business trust, legal representatives, or any organized groups of persons.

(b) The term "employer" means a person engaged in an industry affecting commerce who has twenty or more employees for each working day in each of twenty or more calendar weeks in the current or preceding calendar year: Provided, That prior to June 30, 1968, employers having fewer than fifty employees shall not be considered employers. The term also means (1) any agent of such a person, and (2) a State or political subdivision of a State and any agency or instrumentality of a State or a political subdivision of a State, and any interstate agency, but such term does not include the United States, or a corporation wholly owned by the Government of the United States.

(c) The term "employment agency" means any person regularly undertaking with or without compensation to procure employees for an employer and includes an agent of such a person; but shall not include an agency of the United States.

(d) The term "labor organization" means a labor organization engaged in an industry affecting commerce, and any agent of such an organization, and includes any organization of any kind, any agency, or employee representation committee, group, association, or plan so engaged in which employees participate and which exists for the purpose, in whole or in part, of dealing with employers concerning grievances, labor disputes, wages, rates of pay, hours, or other terms or conditions of employment, and any conference, general committee, joint or system board, or joint council so engaged which is subordinate to a national or international labor organization.

(e) A labor organization shall be deemed to be engaged in an industry affecting commerce if (1) it maintains or operates a hiring hall or hiring office which procures employees for an employer or procures for employees opportunities to work for an employer, or (2) the number of its members (or, where it is a labor organization composed of other labor organizations or their representatives, if the aggregate number of the members of such other labor organization) is fifty or more prior to July 1, 1968, or twenty-five or more on or after July 1, 1968, and such labor organization—

(1) is the certified representative of employees under the provisions of the National Labor Relations Act, as amended [29 U.S.C.A. § 151 et seq.], or the Railway Labor Act, as amended [45 U.S.C.A. § 151 et seq.]; or

(2) although not certified, is a national or international labor organization or a local labor organization recognized or acting as the representative of employees of an employer or employers engaged in an industry affecting commerce; or

(3) has chartered a local labor organization or subsidiary body which is representing or actively seeking to represent employees of employers within the meaning of paragraph (1) or (2); or

(4) has been chartered by a labor organization representing or actively seeking to represent employees within the meaning of paragraph (1) or (2) as the local or subordinate body through which such employees may enjoy membership or become affiliated with such labor organization; or

(5) is a conference, general committee, joint or system board, or joint council subordinate to a national or international labor organization, which includes a labor organization engaged in an industry affecting commerce within the meaning of any of the preceding paragraphs of this subsection.

(f) The term "employee" means an individual employed by any employer except that the term "employee" shall not include any person elected to public office in any State or political subdivision of any State by the qualified voters thereof, or any person chosen by such officer to be on such officer's personal staff, or an appointee on the policymaking level or an immediate adviser with respect to the exercise of the constitutional or legal powers of the office. The exemption set forth in the preceding sentence shall not include employees subject to the civil service laws of a State government, governmental agency, or political subdivision. The term "employee" includes any individual who is a citizen of the United States employed by an employer in a workplace in a foreign country.

(g) The term "commerce" means trade, traffic, commerce, transportation, transmission, or communication among the several States; or between a State and any place outside thereof; or within the District of

Columbia, or a possession of the United States; or between points in the same State but through a point outside thereof.

(h) The term "industry affecting commerce" means any activity, business, or industry in commerce or in which a labor dispute would hinder or obstruct commerce or the free flow of commerce and includes any activity or industry "affecting commerce" within the meaning of the Labor–Management Reporting and Disclosure Act of 1959 [29 U.S.C.A. § 401 et seq.].

(i) The term "State" includes a State of the United States, the District of Columbia, Puerto Rico, the Virgin Islands, American Samoa, Guam, Wake Island, the Canal Zone, and Outer Continental Shelf lands defined in the Outer Continental Shelf Lands Act [43 U.S.C.A. § 1331 et seq.].

(j) The term "firefighter" means an employee, the duties of whose position are primarily to perform work directly connected with the control and extinguishment of fires or the maintenance and use of firefighting apparatus and equipment, including an employee engaged in this activity who is transferred to a supervisory or administrative position.

(k) The term "law enforcement officer" means an employee, the duties of whose position are primarily the investigation, apprehension, or detention of individuals suspected or convicted of offenses against the criminal laws of a State, including an employee engaged in this activity who is transferred to a supervisory or administrative position. For the purpose of this subsection, "detention" includes the duties of employees assigned to guard individuals incarcerated in any penal institution.

(*l*) The term "compensation, terms, conditions, or privileges of employment" encompasses all employee benefits, including such benefits provided pursuant to a bona fide employee benefit plan.

§ 631. Age limits

(a) Individuals at least 40

The prohibitions in this chapter shall be limited to individuals who are at least 40 years of age.

(b) Employees or applicants for employment in Federal Government

In the case of any personnel action affecting employees or applicants for employment which is subject to the provisions of section 633a of this title, the prohibitions established in section 633a of this title shall be limited to individuals who are at least 40 years of age.

(c) Bona fide executives or high policymakers

(1) Nothing in this chapter shall be construed to prohibit compulsory retirement of any employee who has attained 65 years of age, and who, for the 2-year period immediately before retirement, is employed in a bona fide executive or a high policymaking position, if such employee is

entitled to an immediate nonforfeitable annual retirement benefit from a pension, profit-sharing, savings, or deferred compensation plan, or any combination of such plans, of the employer of such employee, which equals, in the aggregate, at least $44,000.

(2) In applying the retirement benefit test of paragraph (1) of this subsection, if any such retirement benefit is in a form other than a straight life annuity (with no ancillary benefits), or if employees contribute to any such plan or make rollover contributions, such benefit shall be adjusted in accordance with regulations prescribed by the Equal Employment Opportunity Commission, after consultation with the Secretary of the Treasury, so that the benefit is the equivalent of a straight life annuity (with no ancillary benefits) under a plan to which employees do not contribute and under which no rollover contributions are made.

* * *

§ 633.   Federal–State relationship

(a) Federal action superseding State action

Nothing in this chapter shall affect the jurisdiction of any agency of any State performing like functions with regard to discriminatory employment practices on account of age except that upon commencement of action under this chapter such action shall supersede any State action.

(b) Limitation of Federal action upon commencement of State proceedings

In the case of an alleged unlawful practice occurring in a State which has a law prohibiting discrimination in employment because of age and establishing or authorizing a State authority to grant or seek relief from such discriminatory practice, no suit may be brought under section 626 of this title before the expiration of sixty days after proceedings have been commenced under the State law, unless such proceedings have been earlier terminated: Provided, That such sixty-day period shall be extended to one hundred and twenty days during the first year after the effective date of such State law. If any requirement for the commencement of such proceedings is imposed by a State authority other than a requirement of the filing of a written and signed statement of the facts upon which the proceeding is based, the proceeding shall be deemed to have been commenced for the purposes of this subsection at the time such statement is sent by registered mail to the appropriate State authority.

§ 633a.   Nondiscrimination on account of age in Federal Government employment

(a) Federal agencies affected

All personnel actions affecting employees or applicants for employment who are at least 40 years of age (except personnel actions with regard to aliens employed outside the limits of the United States) in military departments as defined in section 102 of Title 5, in executive agencies as defined in section 105 of Title 5 (including employees and applicants for employment who are paid from nonappropriated funds), in the United States Postal Service and the Postal Rate Commission, in those units in the government of the District of Columbia having positions in the competitive service, and in those units of the judicial branch of the Federal Government having positions in the competitive service, and in the Government Printing Office, the General Accounting Office, and the Library of Congress shall be made free from any discrimination based on age.

(b) Enforcement by Equal Employment Opportunity Commission and by Librarian of Congress in the Library of Congress; remedies; rules, regulations, orders, and instructions of Commission: compliance by Federal agencies; powers and duties of Commission; notification of final action on complaint of discrimination; exemptions: bona fide occupational qualification

Except as otherwise provided in this subsection, the Equal Employment Opportunity Commission is authorized to enforce the provisions of subsection (a) of this section through appropriate remedies, including reinstatement or hiring of employees with or without backpay, as will effectuate the policies of this section. The Equal Employment Opportunity Commission shall issue such rules, regulations, orders, and instructions as it deems necessary and appropriate to carry out its responsibilities under this section. The Equal Employment Opportunity Commission shall—

(1) be responsible for the review and evaluation of the operation of all agency programs designed to carry out the policy of this section, periodically obtaining and publishing (on at least a semiannual basis) progress reports from each department, agency, or unit referred to in subsection (a) of this section;

(2) consult with and solicit the recommendations of interested individuals, groups, and organizations relating to nondiscrimination in employment on account of age; and

(3) provide for the acceptance and processing of complaints of discrimination in Federal employment on account of age.

The head of each such department, agency, or unit shall comply with such rules, regulations, orders, and instructions of the Equal Employment Opportunity Commission which shall include a provision that an employee or applicant for employment shall be notified of any final action taken on any complaint of discrimination filed by him thereunder. Reasonable exemptions to the provisions of this section may be established by the Commission but only when the Commission has established a maximum age requirement on the basis of a determination that age is a bona fide occupational qualification necessary to the performance of the duties of the position. With respect to employment in the Library of Congress, authorities granted in this subsection to the Equal Employment Opportunity Commission shall be exercised by the Librarian of Congress.

(c) Civil actions; jurisdiction; relief

Any person aggrieved may bring a civil action in any Federal district court of competent jurisdiction for such legal or equitable relief as will effectuate the purposes of this chapter.

(d) Notice to Commission; time of notice; Commission notification of prospective defendants; Commission elimination of unlawful practices

When the individual has not filed a complaint concerning age discrimination with the Commission, no civil action may be commenced by any individual under this section until the individual has given the Commission not less than thirty days' notice of an intent to file such action. Such notice shall be filed within one hundred and eighty days after the alleged unlawful practice occurred. Upon receiving a notice of intent to sue, the Commission shall promptly notify all persons named therein as prospective defendants in the action and take any appropriate action to assure the elimination of any unlawful practice.

(e) Duty of Government agency or official

Nothing contained in this section shall relieve any Government agency or official of the responsibility to assure nondiscrimination on account of age in employment as required under any provision of Federal law.

(f) Applicability of statutory provisions to personnel action of Federal departments, etc.

Any personnel action of any department, agency, or other entity referred to in subsection (a) of this section shall not be subject to, or affected by, any provision of this chapter, other than the provisions of section 631(b) of this title and the provisions of this section. * * *

AGE DISCRIMINATION IN EMPLOYMENT AMENDMENTS OF 1986

[The 1986 amendments removed the maximum age limit of seventy years old and thus prohibited discrimination against anyone forty years of age or older. At the same time Congress added the following exceptions for temporary exemptions to this change in coverage. The time limitation on these exceptions has now expired, but bills introduced in the 104th Congress are currently being considered for the purpose of reinstating the exemption for firefighting and law enforcement officers.]

§ 3.   Employment as Firefighting or Law Enforcement Officer.

(a) General Rule.—Section 4 of the Age Discrimination in Employment Act of 1967 (29 U.S.C. § 623) is amended by adding at the end thereof the following new subsection:

"(i) It shall not be unlawful for an employer which is a State, a political subdivision of a State, an agency or instrumentality of a State or a political subdivision of a State, or an interstate agency to fail or refuse to hire or to discharge any individual because of such individual's age if such action is taken—

"(1) with respect to the employment of an individual as a firefighter or as a law enforcement officer and the individual has attained the age of hiring or retirement in effect under applicable State or local law on March 3, 1983, and

"(2) pursuant to a bona fide hiring or retirement plan that is not a subterfuge to evade the purposes of this Act.".

(b) Termination Provision.—The amendment made by subsection (a) of this section is repealed December 31, 1993.

§ 4.   Definitions.

Section 11 of the Age Discrimination in Employment Act of 1967 (29 U.S.C. § 630) is amended by adding at the end thereof the following new subsections:

"(j) The term 'firefighter' means an employee, the duties of whose position are primarily to perform work directly connected with the control and extinguishment of fires or the maintenance and use of firefighting apparatus and equipment, including an employee engaged in this activity who is transferred to a supervisory or administrative position.

"(k) The term 'law enforcement officer' means an employee, the duties of whose position are primarily the investigation, apprehension, or detention of individuals suspected or convicted of offenses against the criminal laws of a State, including an employee engaged in this activity who is transferred to a supervisory or administrative position. For the purpose of this subsection, 'detention' includes the duties of employees assigned to guard individuals incarcerated in any penal institution.".

* * *

§ 6.   Special Rule for Tenure Faculty.

(a) Special Rule.—Section 12 of the Age Discrimination in Employment Act of 1967 (29 U.S.C. § 631) is amended by adding at the end thereof the following new subsection:

"(d) Nothing in this Act shall be construed to prohibit compulsory retirement of any employee who has attained 70 years of age, and who is serving under a contract of unlimited tenure (or similar arrangement providing for unlimited tenure) at any institution of higher education (as defined by section 1201(a) of the Higher Education Act of 1965).".

(b) Termination Provision.—The amendment made by subsection (a) of this section is repealed December 31, 1993.

* * *

AMERICANS WITH DISABILITIES ACT

104 Stat. 327 (1990), as amended 105 Stat. 1071 (1991), 109 Stat. 3 (1995)

[The Americans with Disabilities Act contains several Titles: Employment, Public Services, Public Accommodations and Services Operated by Private Entities, and Miscellaneous Provisions. Excerpted below are portions relevant to employment discrimination.]

§ 12101.   Findings and Purposes (§ 2)

(a) Findings.

Congress finds that—

(1) some 43,000,000 Americans have one or more physical or mental disabilities, and this number is increasing as the population as a whole is growing older;

(2) historically, society has tended to isolate and segregate individuals with disabilities, and, despite some improvements, such forms of discrimination against individuals with disabilities continue to be a serious and pervasive social problem;

(3) discrimination against individuals with disabilities persists in such critical areas as employment, housing, public accommodations, education, transportation, communication, recreation, institutionalization, health services, voting, and access to public services;

(4) unlike individuals who have experienced discrimination on the basis of race, sex, national origin, religion, or age, individuals who have experienced discrimination on the basis of disability have often had no legal recourse to redress such discrimination;

(5) individuals with disabilities continually encounter various forms of discrimination, including outright intentional exclusion, the discriminatory effects of architectural, transportation, and communication barriers, over-protective rules and policies, failure to make modifications to existing facilities and practices, exclusionary qualification standards and criteria, segregation, and relegation to lesser services, programs, activities, benefits, jobs, or other opportunities;

(6) census data, national polls, and other studies have documented that people with disabilities, as a group, occupy an inferior status in our society, and are severely disadvantaged socially, vocationally, economically, and educationally;

(7) individuals with disabilities are a discrete and insular minority who have been faced with restrictions and limitations, subjected to a history of purposeful unequal treatment, and relegated to a position of political powerlessness in our society, based on characteristics that are beyond the control of such individuals and resulting from stereotypic assumptions not truly indicative of the individual ability of such individuals to participate in, and contribute to, society;

(8) the Nation's proper goals regarding individuals with disabilities are to assure equality of opportunity, full participation, independent living, and economic self-sufficiency for such individuals; and

(9) the continuing existence of unfair and unnecessary discrimination and prejudice denies people with disabilities the opportunity to compete on an equal basis and to pursue those opportunities for which our free society is justifiably famous, and costs the United States billions of dollars in unnecessary expenses resulting from dependency and non-productivity.

(b) Purpose.

It is the purpose of this Act—

(1) to provide a clear and comprehensive national mandate for the elimination of discrimination against individuals with disabilities;

(2) to provide clear, strong, consistent, enforceable standards addressing discrimination against individuals with disabilities;

(3) to ensure that the Federal Government plays a central role in enforcing the standards established in this Act on behalf of individuals with disabilities; and

(4) to invoke the sweep of congressional authority, including its power to enforce the fourteenth amendment and to regulate commerce, in order to address the major areas of discrimination faced day-to-day by people with disabilities.

§ 12102. Definitions (§ 3)

(1) Auxiliary Aids and Services.—The term "auxiliary aids and services includes—

(A) qualified interpreters or other effective methods of making aurally delivered materials available to individuals with hearing impairments;

(B) qualified readers, taped texts, or other effective methods of making visually delivered materials available to individuals with visual impairments;

(C) acquisition or modification of equipment or devices; and

(D) other similar services and actions.

(2) Disability.—The term "disability" means, with respect to an individual—

(A) a physical or mental impairment that substantially limits one or more of the major life activities of such individual;

(B) a record of such an impairment; or

(C) being regarded as having such an impairment.

(3) State.—The term "State" means each of the several States, the District of Columbia, the Commonwealth of Puerto Rico, Guam, Ameri-

can Samoa, the Virgin Islands, the Trust Territory of the Pacific Islands, and the Commonwealth of the Northern Mariana Islands.

TITLE I—EMPLOYMENT

§ 12111. Definitions (§ 101)

As used in this title:

(1) Commission.—The term "Commission" means the Equal Employment Opportunity Commission established by section 705 of the Civil Rights Act of 1964 (42 U.S.C. 2000e–4).

(2) Covered Entity.—The term "covered entity" means an employer, employment agency, labor organization, or joint labor-management committee.

(3) Direct Threat.—The term "direct threat" means a significant risk to the health or safety of others that cannot be eliminated by reasonable accommodation.

(4) Employee.—The term "employee" means an individual employed by an employer. With respect to employment in a foreign country, such term includes an individual who is a citizen of the United States. [This provision does not apply to conduct occurring before November 21, 1991.—Eds.]

(5) Employer.—

(A) The term "employer" means a person engaged in an industry affecting commerce who has 15 or more employees for each working day in each of 20 or more calendar weeks in the current or preceding calendar year, and any agent of such person, except that, for two years following the effective date of this title, an employer means a person engaged in an industry affecting commerce who has 25 or more employees for each working day in each of 20 or more calendar weeks in the current or preceding year, and any agent of such person.

(B) Exceptions.—The term "employer" does not include

(i) the United States, a corporation wholly owned by the government of the United States, or an Indian tribe; or

(ii) a bona fide private membership club (other than a labor organization) that is exempt from taxation under section 501(c) of the Internal Revenue Code of 1986.

(6) Illegal Use of Drugs.

(A) In General.

The term "illegal use of drugs" means the use of drugs, the possession or distribution of which is unlawful under the Controlled Substances Act (21 U.S.C. 812). Such term does not include the use of a drug taken under supervision by a licensed health care professional or other uses authorized by the Controlled Substances Act or other provisions of Federal law.

(B) Drugs.

The term "drug" means a controlled substance, as defined in schedules I through V of section 202 of the Controlled Substances Act.

(7) Person, etc.—The terms "person," "labor organization," "employment agency," "commerce," and "industry affecting commerce," shall have the same meaning given such terms in section 701 of the Civil Rights Act of 1964 (42 U.S.C. 2000e).

(8) Qualified Individual With A Disability.—The term "qualified individual with a disability" means an individual with a disability who, with or without reasonable accommodation, can perform the essential functions of the employment position that such individual holds or desires. For the purposes of this title, consideration shall be given to the employer's judgment as to what functions of a job are essential, and if an employer has prepared a written description before advertising or interviewing applicants for the job, this description shall be considered evidence of the essential functions of the job.

(9) Reasonable Accommodation.—The term "reasonable accommodation" may include—

(A) making existing facilities used by employees readily accessible to and usable by individuals with disabilities; and

(B) job restructuring, part-time or modified work schedules, reassignment to a vacant position, acquisition or modification of equipment or devices, appropriate adjustment or modifications of examinations, training materials or policies, the provision of qualified readers or interpreters, and other similar accommodations for individuals with disabilities.

(10) Undue Hardship.

(A) In General.—The term "undue hardship" means an action requiring significant difficulty or expense, when considered in light of the factors set forth in subparagraph (B).

(B) Factors To Be Considered.—In determining whether an accommodation would impose an undue hardship on a covered entity, factors to be considered include—

(i) the nature and cost of the accommodation needed under this Act;

(ii) the overall financial resources of the facility or facilities involved in the provision of the reasonable accommodation; the number of persons employed at such facility; the effect on expenses and resources, or the impact otherwise of such accommodation upon the operation of the facility;

(iii) the overall financial resources of the covered entity; the overall size of the business of a covered entity with respect to the number of its employees; the number, type, and location of its facilities; and

(iv) the type of operation or operations of the covered entity, including the composition, structure, and functions of the workforce of such entity; the geographic separateness, administrative, or fiscal relationship of the facility or facilities in question to the covered entity.

§ 12112.   Discrimination (§ 102)

(a) General Rule.

No covered entity shall discriminate against a qualified individual with a disability because of the disability of such individual in regard to job application procedures, the hiring, advancement, or discharge of employees, employee compensation, job training, and other terms, conditions, and privileges of employment.

(b) Construction.

As used in subsection (a), the term "discrimination" includes—

(1) limiting, segregating, or classifying a job applicant or employee in a way that adversely affects the opportunities or status of such applicant or employee because of the disability of such applicant or employee;

(2) participating in a contractual or other arrangement or relationship that has the effect of subjecting a covered entity's qualified applicant or employee with a disability to the discrimination prohibited by this title (such relationship includes a relationship with an employment or referral agency, labor union, an organization providing fringe benefits to an employee of the covered entity, or an organization providing training and apprenticeship programs);

(3) utilizing standards, criteria, or methods of administration—

(A) that have the effect of discrimination on the basis of disability; or

(B) that perpetuate the discrimination of others who are subject to common administrative control;

(4) excluding or otherwise denying equal jobs or benefits to a qualified individual because of the known disability of an individual with whom the qualified individual is known to have a relationship or association;

(5)(A) not making reasonable accommodations to the known physical or mental limitations of a qualified individual who is an applicant or employee, unless such covered entity can demonstrate that the accommodation would impose an undue hardship on the operation of the business of such covered entity;

(B) denying employment opportunities to a job applicant or employee who is a qualified individual with a disability, if such denial is based on the need of such covered entity to make reasonable accommodation to the physical or mental impairments of the employee or applicant;

(6) using qualification standards, employment tests or other selection criteria that screen out or tend to screen out an individual with a disability or a class of individuals with disabilities unless the standard, test or other selection criteria, as used by the covered entity, is shown to be job-related for the position in question and is consistent with business necessity; and

(7) failing to select and administer tests concerning employment in the most effective manner to ensure that, when such test is administered to a job applicant or employee who has a disability that impairs sensory, manual, or speaking skills, such test results accurately reflect the skills, aptitude, or whatever other factor of such applicant or employee that such test purports to measure, rather than reflecting the impaired sensory, manual, or speaking skills of such employee or applicant (except where such skills are the factors that the test purports to measure).

(c) Covered Entities In Foreign Countries.

(1) In General.—It shall not be unlawful under this section for a covered entity to take any action that constitutes discrimination under this section with respect to an employee in a workplace in a foreign country if compliance with this section would cause such covered entity to violate the law of the foreign country in which such workplace is located.

(2) Control of Corporation.

(A) Presumption. If an employer controls a corporation whose place of incorporation is a foreign country, any practice that constitutes discrimination under this section and is engaged in by such corporation shall be presumed to be engaged in by such employer.

(B) Exception. This section shall not apply with respect to the foreign operations of an employer that is a foreign person not controlled by an American employer.

(C) Determination. For purposes of this para-graph, the determination of whether an employer controls a corporation shall be based on—

(i) the interrelation of operations;

(ii) the common management;

(iii) the centralized control of labor relations; and

(iv) the common ownership or financial control of the employer and the corporation. [This provision does not apply to conduct occurring before November 21, 1991.—Eds.]

(d) Medical Examinations and Inquiries.

(1) In General.—The prohibition against discrimination as referred to in subsection (a) shall include medical examinations and inquiries.

(2) Preemployment.—

(A) Prohibited Examination or Inquiry.—Except as provided in paragraph (3), a covered entity shall not conduct a medical examination or make inquiries of a job applicant or employee as to whether such applicant or employee is an individual with a disability or as to the nature of severity of such disability.

(B) Acceptable Inquiry.—A covered entity may make preemployment inquiries into the ability of an applicant to perform job-related functions.

(3) Employment Entrance Examination.—A covered entity may require a medical examination after an offer of employment has been made to a job applicant and prior to the commencement of the employment duties of such applicant, and may condition an offer of employment on the results of such examination, if—

(A) all entering employees are subjected to such an examination regardless of disability;

(B) information obtained regarding the medical condition or history of the applicant is collected and maintained on separate forms and in separate medical files and is treated as a confidential medical record, except that—

(i) supervisors and managers may be informed regarding necessary restrictions on the work or duties of the employee and necessary accommodations;

(ii) first aid and safety personnel may be informed, when appropriate, if the disability might require emergency treatment; and

(iii) government officials investigating compliance with this Act shall be provided relevant information on request; and

(C) the results of such examination are used only in accordance with this title.

(4) Examination and Inquiry.—

(A) Prohibited Examinations and Inquiries.—A covered entity shall require a medical examination and shall not make inquiries of an employee as to whether such employee is an individual with a disability or as to the nature or severity of the disability, unless such examination or inquiry is shown to be job-related and consistent with business necessity.

(B) Acceptable Inquiries.—A covered entity may conduct voluntary medical examinations, including voluntary medical histories, which are part of an employee health program available to employees at that work site. A covered entity may make inquiries into the ability of an employee to perform job-related functions.

(C) Requirement.—Information obtained under subparagraph (B) regarding the medical condition or history of any employee are subject to the requirements of subparagraphs (B) and (C) of paragraph (3).

§ 12113. Defenses (§ 103)

(a) In General.

It may be a defense to a charge of discrimination under this Act that an alleged application of qualification standards, tests, or selection criteria that screen out or tend to screen out or otherwise deny a job or benefit to an individual with a disability has been shown to be job-related and consistent with business necessity, and such performance cannot be accomplished by reasonable accommodation, as required under this title.

(b) Qualification Standards.

The term "qualification standards" may include a requirement that an individual shall not pose a direct threat to the health or safety or other individuals in the workplace.

(c) Religious Entities.

(1) In General.—This title shall not prohibit a religious corporation, association, educational institution, or society from giving preference in employment to individuals of a particular religion to perform work connected with the carrying on by such corporation, association, educational institution, or society of its activities.

(2) Religious Tenets Requirement.—Under this title, a religious organization may require that all applicants and employees conform to the religious tenets of such organization.

(d) List of Infectious and Communicable Diseases.

(1) In General.—The Secretary of Health and Human Services, not later than 6 months after the date of enactment of this Act, shall—

(A) review all infectious and communicable diseases which may be transmitted through handling the food supply;

(B) publish a list of infectious and communicable diseases which are transmitted through handling the food supply;

(C) publish the methods by which such diseases are transmitted; and

(D) widely disseminate such information regarding the list of diseases and their modes of transmissibility to the general public.

(2) Applications.—In any case in which an individual has an infectious or communicable disease that is transmitted to others through the handling of food, that is included on the list developed by the Secretary of Health and Human Services under paragraph

(1), and which cannot be eliminated by reasonable accommodation, a covered entity may refuse to assign or continue to assign such individual to a job involving food handling.

(3) Construction.—Nothing in this Act shall be construed to preempt, modify, or amend any state, county, or local law, ordinance, or regulation applicable to food handling which is designed to protect the public health from individuals who pose a significant risk to the health or safety of others, which cannot be eliminated by reasonable accommodation, pursuant to the list of infectious or communicable diseases and the modes of transmissibility published by the Secretary of Health and Human Services.

§ 12114.   Illegal Druge and Alcohol (§ 104)

(a) Qualified Individual With A Disability.

For purposes of this title, the term "qualified individual with a disability" shall not include any employee or applicant who is currently engaging in the illegal use of drugs, when the covered entity acts on the basis of such use.

(b) Rules of Construction.

Nothing in subsection (a) shall be construed to exclude as a qualified individual with a disability an individual who—

(1) has successfully completed a supervised drug rehabilitation program and is no longer engaging in the illegal use of drugs, or has otherwise been rehabilitated successfully and is no longer engaging in such use;

(2) is participating in a supervised rehabilitation program and is no longer engaging in such use; or

(3) is erroneously regarded as engaging in such use, but is not engaging in such use;

except that it shall not be a violation of this Act for a covered entity to adopt or administer reasonable policies or procedures, including but not limited to drug testing, designed to ensure that an individual described in paragraph (1) or (2) is no longer engaging in the illegal use of drugs.

(c) Authority of Covered Entity.

A covered entity—

(1) may prohibit the illegal use of drugs and the use of alcohol at the workplace by all employees;

(2) may require that employees shall not be under the influence of alcohol or be engaging in the illegal use of drugs at the workplace;

(3) may require that employees behave in conformance with the requirements established under the Drug–Free Workplace Act of 1988 (41 U.S.C. 701 et seq.);

(4) may hold an employee who engages in the illegal use of drugs or who is an alcoholic to the same qualification standards for

employment or job performance and behavior that such entity holds other employees, even if any unsatisfactory performance or behavior is related to the drug use or alcoholism of such employee; and

(5) may, with respect to Federal regulations regarding alcohol and the illegal use of drugs, require that—

(A) employees comply with the standards established in such regulations of the Department of Defense, if the employees of the covered entity are employed in an industry subject to such regulations, including complying with regulations (if any) that apply to employment in sensitive positions in such an industry, in the case of employees of the covered entity who are employed in such positions (as defined in the regulations of the Department of Defense);

(B) employees comply with the standards established in such regulations of the Nuclear Regulatory Commission, if the employees of the covered entity are employed in an industry subject to such regulations, including complying with regulations (if any) that apply to employment in sensitive positions in such an industry, in the case of employees of the covered entity who are employed in such positions (as defined in the regulations of the Nuclear Regulatory Commission); and

(C) employees comply with the standards established in such regulations of the Department of Transportation, if the employees of the covered entity are employed in a transportation industry subject to such regulations, including complying with such regulations (if any) that apply to employment in sensitive positions in such an industry, in the case of employees of the covered entity who are employed in such positions (as defined in the regulations of the Department of Transportation).

(d) Drug Testing.

(1) In General.—For purposes of this title, a test to determine the illegal use of drugs shall not be considered a medical examination.

(2) Construction.—Nothing in this title shall be construed to encourage, prohibit, or authorize the conducting of drug testing for the illegal use of drugs by job applicants or employees or making employment decisions based on such test results.

(e) Transportation Employees.

Nothing in this title shall be construed to encourage, prohibit, restrict, or authorize the otherwise lawful exercise by entities subject to the jurisdiction of the Department of Transportation of authority to—

(1) test employees of such entities in, and applicants for, positions involving safety-sensitive duties for the illegal use of drugs and for on-duty impairment by alcohol; and

(2) remove such persons who test positive for illegal use of drugs and on-duty impairment by alcohol pursuant to paragraph (1) from safety-sensitive duties in implementing subsection (c).

§ 12115. Posting Notices (§ 105)

Every employer, employment agency, labor organization, or joint labor-management committee covered under this title shall post notices in an accessible format to applicants, employees, and members describing the applicable provisions of this Act, in the manner prescribed by section 711 of the Civil Rights Act of 1964 (42 U.S.C. 2000e–10).

§ 12116. Regulations (§ 106)

Not later than 1 year after the date of enactment of this Act, the Commission shall issue regulations in an accessible format to carry out this title in accordance with subchapter II of chapter 5 of title 5, United States Code.

§ 12117. Enforcement (§ 107)

(a) Powers, Remedies, and Procedures.

The powers, remedies, and procedures set forth in sections 705, 706, 707, 709, and 710 of the Civil Rights Act of 1964 (42 U.S.C. 2000e–4, 2000e–5, 2000e–6, 2000e–8, and 2000e–9) shall be the powers, remedies, and procedures this title provides to the Commission, to the Attorney General, or to any person alleging discrimination on the basis of disability in violation of any provision of this Act, or regulations promulgated under section 106, concerning employment.

(b) Coordination.

The agencies with enforcement authority for actions which allege employment discrimination under this title and under the Rehabilitation Act of 1973 shall develop procedures to ensure that administrative complaints filed under this title and under the Rehabilitation Act of 1973 are dealt with in a manner that avoids duplication of effort and prevents imposition of inconsistent or conflicting standards for the same requirements under this title and the Rehabilitation Act of 1973. The Commission, the Attorney General, and the Office of Federal Contract Compliance Programs shall establish such coordinating mechanisms (similar to provisions contained in the joint regulations promulgated by the Commission and the Attorney General at part 42 of title 28 and part 1691 of title 29, Code of Federal Regulations, and the Memorandum of Understanding between the Commission and the Office of Federal Contract Compliance Programs dated January 16, 1981 (46 Fed. Reg. 7435, January 23, 1981)) in regulations implementing this title and Rehabilitation Act of 1973 not later than 18 months after the date of enactment of this Act.

§ 12118. Effective Date § 108

This title shall become effective 24 months after the date of enactment.

TITLE V—MISCELLANEOUS PROVISIONS

§ 12201. Construction (§ 501)

(a) In General.

Except as otherwise provided in this Act, nothing in this Act shall be construed to apply a lesser standard than the standards applied under title V of the Rehabilitation Act of 1973 (29 U.S.C. 790 et seq.) or the regulations issued by Federal agencies pursuant to such title.

(b) Relationship to Other Laws.

Nothing in this Act shall be construed to invalidate or limit the remedies, rights, and procedures of any Federal law or law of any State or political subdivision of any State or jurisdiction that provides greater or equal protection for the rights of individuals with disabilities than are afforded by this Act. Nothing in this Act shall be construed to preclude the prohibition of, or the imposition of restrictions on, smoking in places of employment covered by title I, in transportation covered by title II or III, or in places of public accommodation covered by title III.

(c) Insurance.

Titles I through IV of this Act shall not be construed to prohibit or restrict—

(1) an insurer, hospital or medical service company, health maintenance organization, or any agent or entity that administers benefit plans, or similar organizations from underwriting risks, classifying risks, or administering such risks that are based on or not inconsistent with State law; or

(2) a person or organization covered by this Act from establishing, sponsoring, observing or administering the terms of a bona fide benefit plan that are based on underwriting risks, classifying risks, or administering such risks that are based on or not inconsistent with State law; or

(3) a person or organization covered by this Act from establishing, sponsoring, observing or administering the terms of a bona fide benefit plan that is not subject to State laws that regulate insurance. Paragraphs (1), (2), and (3) shall not be used as a subterfuge to evade the purposes of title I and III.

(d) Accommodations and Services.

Nothing in this Act shall be construed to require an individual with a disability to accept an accommodation, aid, service, opportunity, or benefit which such individual chooses not to accept.

§ 12202. State Immunity (§ 502)

A State shall not be immune under the eleventh amendment to the Constitution of the United States from an action in Federal or State court of competent jurisdiction for a violation of this Act. In any action against a State for a violation of the requirements of this Act, remedies (including remedies both at law and in equity) are available for such a violation to the same extent as such remedies are available for such a violation in an action against any public or private entity other than a State.

§ 12203. Prohibition Against Retaliation and Coercion (§ 503)

(a) Retaliation.

No person shall discriminate against any individual because such individual has opposed any act or practice made unlawful by this Act or because such individual made a charge, testified, assisted, or participated in any manner in an investigation, proceeding, or hearing under this Act.

(b) Interference, Coercion, or Intimidation.

It shall be unlawful to coerce, intimidate, threaten, or interfere with any individual in the exercise or enjoyment of, or on account of his or her having exercised or enjoyed, or on account of his or her having aided or encouraged any other individual in the exercise or enjoyment of, any right granted or protected by this Act.

(c) Remedies and Procedures.

The remedies and procedures available under sections 107, 203, and 308 of this Act shall be available to aggrieved persons for violations of subsections (a) and (b), with respect to title I, title II and title III, respectively.

§ 12205. Attorney's Fees (§ 505)

In any action or administrative proceeding commenced pursuant to this Act, the court or agency, in its discretion, may allow the prevailing party, other than the United States, a reasonable attorney's fee, including litigation expenses, and costs, and the United States shall be liable for the foregoing the same as a private individual.

§ 12208. Transvestites (§ 508)

For purposes of this Act, the term "disabled" or "disability" shall not apply to an individual solely because that individual is a transvestite.

* * *

§ 12210. Illegal Use of Drugs (§ 510)

(a) In General.

For purposes of this Act, the term "individual with a disability" does not include an individual who is currently engaging in the illegal use of drugs, when the covered entity acts on the basis of such use.

(b) Rules of Construction.

Nothing in subsection (a) shall be construed to exclude as an individual with a disability an individual who—

(1) has successfully completed a supervised drug rehabilitation program and is no longer engaging in the illegal use of drugs, or has otherwise been rehabilitated successfully and is no longer engaging in such use;

(2) is participating in a supervised rehabilitation program and is no longer engaging in such use; or

(3) is erroneously regarded as engaging in such use, but is not engaging in such use;

except that it shall not be a violation of this Act for a covered entity to adopt or administer reasonable policies or procedures, including but not limited to drug testing, designed to ensure that an individual described in paragraph (1) or (2) is no longer engaging in the illegal use of drugs; however, nothing in this section shall be construed to encourage, prohibit, restrict, or authorize the conducting of testing for the illegal use of drugs.

(c) Health and Other Services.

Notwithstanding subsection (a) and section 511(b)(3), an individual shall not be denied health services, or services provided in connection with drug rehabilitation, on the basis of the current illegal use of drugs if the individual is otherwise entitled to such services.

(d) Definition of Illegal Use of Drugs.

(1) In General.—The term "illegal use of drugs" means the use of drugs, the possession or distribution of which is unlawful under the Controlled Substances Act (21 U.S.C. 812). Such term does not include the use of a drug taken under supervision by a licensed health care professional, or other uses authorized by the Controlled Substances Act or other provisions of Federal law.

(2) Drugs.—The term "drug" means a controlled substance, as defined in schedules I through V of section 202 of the Controlled Substances Act.

§ 12211.   Definitions (§ 511)

(a) Homosexuality and Bisexuality.

For purposes of the definition of "disability" in section 3(2), homosexuality and bisexuality are not impairments and as such are not disabilities under this Act.

(b) Certain Conditions.

Under this Act, the term "disability" shall not include—

(1) transvestism, transsexualism, pedophilia, exhibitionism, voyeurism, gender identity disorders not resulting from physical impairments, or other sexual behavior disorders;

(2) compulsive gambling, kleptomania, or pyromania; or

(3) psychoactive substance use disorders resulting from current illegal use of drugs.

§ 12212. Alternative Means of Dispute Resolution (§ 513)

Where appropriate and to the extent authorized by law, the use of alternative means of dispute resolution, including settlement negotiations, conciliation, facilitation, mediation, factfinding, minitrials, and arbitration, is encouraged to resolve disputes arising under this Act.

§ 12213. Severability (§ 514)

Should any provision in this Act be found to be unconstitutional by a court of law, such provision shall be severed from the remainder of the Act, and such action shall not affect the enforceability of the remaining provisions of the Act.

EXCERPTS FROM
FAIR LABOR STANDARDS ACT
INCLUDING
THE EQUAL PAY ACT
AND
THE PORTAL–TO–PORTAL ACT

29 U.S.C.A. § 201 et seq.

§ 203. Definitions

As used in this chapter—

(a) "Person" means an individual, partnership, association, corporation, business trust, legal representative, or any organized group of persons.

(b) "Commerce" means trade, commerce, transportation, transmission, or communication among the several States or between any State and any place outside thereof.

(c) "State" means any State of the United States or the District of Columbia or any Territory or possession of the United States.

(d) "Employer" includes any person acting directly or indirectly in the interest of an employer in relation to an employee and includes a public agency, but does not include any labor organization (other than when acting as an employer) or anyone acting in the capacity of officer or agent of such labor organization.

(e)(1) Except as provided in paragraphs (2) and (3), the term "employee" means any individual employed by an employer.

(2) In the case of an individual employed by a public agency, such term means—

(A) any individual employed by the Government of the United States—

(i) as a civilian in the military departments (as defined in section 102 of Title 5),

(ii) in any executive agency (as defined in section 105 of such title),

(iii) in any unit of the legislative or judicial branch of the Government which has positions in the competitive service,

(iv) in a nonappropriated fund instrumentality under the jurisdiction of the Armed Forces, or

(v) in the Library of Congress;

(B) any individual employed by the United States Postal Service or the Postal Rate Commission; and

(C) any individual employed by a State, political subdivision of a State, or an interstate governmental agency, other than such an individual—

(i) who is not subject to the civil service laws of the State, political subdivision, or agency which employs him; and

(ii) who—

(I) holds a public elective office of that State, political subdivision, or agency,

(II) is selected by the holder of such an office to be a member of his personal staff,

(III) is appointed by such an officeholder to serve on a policymaking level, or

(IV) who is an immediate adviser to such an officeholder with respect to the constitutional or legal powers of his office.

(3) For purposes of subsection (u) of this section, such term does not include any individual employed by an employer engaged in agriculture if such individual is the parent, spouse, child, or other member of the employer's immediate family.

* * *

(g) "Employ" includes to suffer or permit to work.

(h) "Industry" means a trade, business, industry, or other activity, or branch or group thereof, in which individuals are gainfully employed.

(i) "Goods" means goods (including ships and marine equipment), wares, products, commodities, merchandise, or articles or subjects of commerce of any character, or any part or ingredient thereof, but does not include goods after their delivery into the actual physical possession of the ultimate consumer thereof other than a producer, manufacturer, or processor thereof.

(j) "Produced" means produced, manufactured, mined, handled, or in any other manner worked on in any State; and for the purposes of this chapter an employee shall be deemed to have been engaged in the production of goods if such employee was employed in producing, manufacturing, mining, handling, transporting, or in any other manner working on such goods, or in any closely related process or occupation directly essential to the production thereof, in any State.

(k) "Sale" or "sell" includes any sale, exchange, contract to sell, consignment for sale, shipment for sale, or other disposition.

* * *

(m) "Wage" paid to any employee includes the reasonable cost, as determined by the Administrator, to the employer of furnishing such employee with board, lodging, or other facilities, if such board, lodging or other facilities are customarily furnished by such employer to his employees: Provided, That the cost of board, lodging, or other facilities shall not be included as a part of the wage paid to any employee to the extent it is excluded therefrom under the terms of a bona fide collective-bargaining agreement applicable to the particular employee: Provided further, That the Secretary is authorized to determine the fair value of such board, lodging, or other facilities for defined classes of employees and in defined areas, based on average cost to the employer or to groups of employers similarly situated, or average value to groups of employees, or other appropriate measures of fair value. Such evaluations, where applicable and pertinent, shall be used in lieu of actual measure of cost in determining the wage paid to any employee. In determining the wage of a tipped employee, the amount paid such employee by his employer shall be deemed to be increased on account of tips by an amount determined by the employer, but not by an amount in excess of 40 per centum of the applicable minimum wage rate, except that the amount of the increase on account of tips determined by the employer may not exceed the value of tips actually received by the employee. The previous sentence shall not apply with respect to any tipped employee unless (1) such employee has been informed by the employer of the provisions of this subsection, and (2) all tips received by such employee have been retained by the employee, except that this subsection shall not be construed to prohibit the pooling of tips among employees who customarily and regularly receive tips.

* * *

(r) "Enterprise" means the related activities performed (either through unified operation or common control) by any person or persons for a common business purpose, and includes all such activities whether performed in one or more establishments or by one or more corporate or other organizational units including departments of an establishment operated through leasing arrangements, but shall not include the related activities performed for such enterprise by an independent contractor: Provided, That, within the meaning of this subsection, a retail or service establishment which is under independent ownership shall not be deemed to be so operated or controlled as to be other than a separate and distinct enterprise by reason of any arrangement, which includes, but is not necessarily limited to, and agreement, (1) that it will sell, or sell only, certain goods specified by a particular manufacturer, distributor, or advertiser, or (2) that it will join with other such establishments in the same industry for the purpose of collective purchasing, or (3) that it will have the exclusive right to sell the goods or use the brand name of a manufacturer, distributor, or advertiser within a specified area, or by reason of the fact that it occupies premises leased to it by a person who also leases premises to other retail or service establishments. For purposes of this subsection, the activities performed by any person or persons—

(1) in connection with the operation of a hospital, an institution primarily engaged in the care of the sick, the aged, the mentally ill

or defective who reside on the premises of such institution, a school for mentally or physically handicapped or gifted children, a pre-school, elementary or secondary school, or an institution of higher education (regardless of whether or not such hospital, institution, or school is public or private or operated for profit or not for profit), or

(2) in connection with the operation of a street, suburban or interurban electric railway, or local trolley or motorbus carrier, if the rates and services of such railway or carrier are subject to regulation by a State or local agency (regardless of whether or not such railway or carrier is public or private or operated for profit or not for profit), or

(3) in connection with the activities of a public agency,

shall be deemed to be activities performed for a business purpose.

(s) "Enterprise engaged in commerce or in the production of goods for commerce" means an enterprise which has employees engaged in commerce or in the production of goods for commerce, or employees handling, selling, or otherwise working on goods or materials that have been moved in or produced for commerce by any person, and which—

(1) during the period February 1, 1967, through January 31, 1969, is an enterprise whose annual gross volume of sales made or business done is not less than $500,000 (exclusive of excise taxes at the retail level which are separately stated) or is a gasoline service establishment whose annual gross volume of sales is not less than $250,000 (exclusive of excise taxes at the retail level which are separately stated), and beginning February 1, 1969, is an enterprise, other than an enterprise which is comprised exclusively of retail or service establishments and which is described in paragraph (2), whose annual gross volume of sales made or business done is not less than $250,000 (exclusive of excise taxes at the retail level which are separately stated);

(2) is an enterprise which is comprised exclusively of one or more retail or service establishments, as defined in section 213(a)(2) of this title, and whose annual gross volume of sales made or business done is not less than $250,000 (exclusive of excise taxes at the retail level which are separately stated), beginning July 1, 1978, whose annual gross volume of sales made or business done is not less than $275,000 (exclusive of excise taxes at the retail level which are separately stated), beginning July 1, 1980, whose annual gross volume of sales made or business done is not less than $325,000 (exclusive of excise taxes at the retail level which are separately stated), and after December 31, 1981, whose annual gross volume of sales made or business done is not less than $362,500 (exclusive of excise taxes at the retail level which are separately stated);

(3) is engaged in laundering, cleaning, or repairing clothing or fabrics;

(4) is engaged in the business of construction or reconstruction, or both;

(5) is engaged in the operation of a hospital, an institution primarily engaged in the care of the sick, the aged, the mentally ill or defective who reside on the premises of such institution, a school for mentally or physically handicapped or gifted children, a pre-school, elementary or secondary school, or an institution of higher education (regardless of whether or not such hospital, institution, or school is public or private or operated for profit or not for profit); or

(6) is an activity of a public agency.

Any establishment which has as its only regular employees the owner thereof or the parent, spouse, child, or other member of the immediate family of such owner shall not be considered to be an enterprise engaged in commerce or in the production of goods for commerce or a part of such an enterprise, and the sales of such establishment shall not be included for the purpose of determining the annual gross volume of sales of any enterprise for the purpose of this subsection. The employees of an enterprise which is a public agency shall for purposes of this subsection be deemed to be employees engaged in commerce, or in the production of goods for commerce, or employees handling, selling, or otherwise working on goods or materials that have been moved in or produced for commerce.

Notwithstanding paragraph (2), an enterprise which is comprised of one or more retail or service establishments, which on June 30, 1978, was subject to section 206(a)(1) of this title, and which because of a change in the dollar volume standard in such paragraph prescribed by the Fair Labor Standards Amendments of 1977 is not subject to such section, shall, if its annual gross volume of sales made or business done is not less than $250,000 (exclusive of excise taxes at the retail level which are separately stated), pay its employees not less than the minimum wage in effect under such section on the day before such change takes effect and shall pay its employees in accordance with section 207 of this title. A violation of the preceding sentence shall be considered a violation of section 206 or 207 of this title, as the case may be.

* * *

§ 206.   Minimum wage

(a) Employees engaged in commerce; home workers in Puerto Rico and Virgin Islands; employees in American Samoa; seamen on American vessels; agricultural employees

Every employer shall pay to each of his employees who in any workweek is engaged in commerce or in the production of goods for commerce, or is employed in an enterprise engaged in commerce or in the production of goods for commerce, wages at the following rates:

* * *

(d) Prohibition of sex discrimination

(1) No employer having employees subject to any provisions of this section shall discriminate, within any establishment in which such employees are employed, between employees on the basis of sex by paying wages to employees in such establishment at a rate less than the rate at which he pays wages to employees of the opposite sex in such establishment for equal work on jobs the performance of which requires equal skill, effort, and responsibility, and which are performed under similar working conditions, except where such payment is made pursuant to (i) a seniority system; (ii) a merit system; (iii) a system which measures earnings by quantity or quality of production; or (iv) a differential based on any other factor other than sex: Provided, That an employer who is paying a wage rate differential in violation of this subsection shall not, in order to comply with the provisions of this subsection, reduce the wage rate of any employee.

(2) No labor organization, or its agents, representing employees of an employer having employees subject to any provisions of this section shall cause or attempt to cause such an employer to discriminate against an employee in violation of paragraph (1) of this subsection.

(3) For purposes of administration and enforcement, any amounts owing to any employee which have been withheld in violation of this subsection shall be deemed to be unpaid minimum wages or unpaid overtime compensation under this chapter.

(4) As used in this subsection, the term "labor organization" means any organization of any kind, or any agency or employee representation committee or plan, in which employees participate and which exists for the purpose, in whole or in part, of dealing with employers concerning grievances, labor disputes, wages, rates of pay, hours of employment, or conditions of work.

§ 207. Maximum hours

(a) Employees engaged in interstate commerce; additional applicability to employees pursuant to subsequent amendatory provisions

* * *

§ 213. Exemptions

* * *

§ 215. Prohibited acts; prima facie evidence

(a) After the expiration of one hundred and twenty days from June 25, 1938, it shall be unlawful for any person—

* * *

(2) to violate any of the provisions of section 206 or section 207 of this title, or any of the provisions of any regulation or order of the Secretary issued under section 214 of this title;

(3) to discharge or in any other manner discriminate against any employee because such employee has filed any complaint or instituted or caused to be instituted any proceeding under or related to this chapter, or has testified or is about to testify in any such proceeding, or has served or is about to serve on an industry committee;

(4) to violate any of the provisions of section 212 of this title;

(5) to violate any of the provisions of section 211(c) of this title, or any regulation or order made or continued in effect under the provisions of section 211(d) of this title, or to make any statement, report, or record filed or kept pursuant to the provisions of such section or of any regulation or order thereunder, knowing such statement, report, or record to be false in a material respect.

* * *

§ 216. Penalties

(a) Fines and imprisonment

* * *

(b) Damages; right of action; attorney's fees and costs; termination of right of action

Any employer who violates the provisions of section 206 or section 207 of this title shall be liable to the employee or employees affected in the amount of their unpaid minimum wages, or their unpaid overtime compensation, as the case may be, and in an additional equal amount as liquidated damages. Any employer who violates the provisions of section 215(a)(3) of this title shall be liable for such legal or equitable relief as may be appropriate to effectuate the purposes of section 215(a)(3) of this title, including without limitation employment, reinstatement, promotion, and the payment of wages lost and an additional equal amount as liquidated damages. An action to recover the liability prescribed in either of the preceding sentences may be maintained against any employer (including a public agency) in any Federal or State court of competent jurisdiction by any one or more employees for and in behalf of himself or themselves and other employees similarly situated. No employee shall be a party plaintiff to any such action unless he gives his consent in writing to become such a party and such consent is filed in the court in which such action is brought. The court in such action shall, in addition to any judgment awarded to the plaintiff or plaintiffs, allow a reasonable attorney's fee to be paid by the defendant, and costs of the action. The right provided by this subsection to bring an action by or on behalf of any employee, and the right of any employee to become a party plaintiff to any such action, shall terminate upon the filing of a complaint by the Secretary of Labor in an action under section 217 of this title in which

(1) restraint is sought of any further delay in the payment of unpaid minimum wages, or the amount of unpaid overtime compensation, as the case may be, owing to such employee under section 206 or section 207 of this title by an employer liable therefor under the provisions of this subsection or (2) legal or equitable relief is sought as a result of alleged violations of section 215(a)(3) of this title.

(c) Payment of wages and compensation; waiver of claims; actions by the Secretary; limitation of actions

The Secretary is authorized to supervise the payment of the unpaid minimum wages on the unpaid overtime compensation owing to any employee or employees under section 206 or section 207 of this title, and the agreement of any employee to accept such payment shall upon payment in full constitute a waiver by such employee of any right he may have under subsection (b) of this section to such unpaid minimum wages or unpaid overtime compensation and an additional equal amount as liquidated damages. The Secretary may bring an action in any court of competent jurisdiction to recover the amount of unpaid minimum wages or overtime compensation and an equal amount as liquidated damages. The right provided by subsection (b) of this section to bring an action by or on behalf of any employee to recover the liability specified in the first sentence of such subsection and of any employee to become a party plaintiff to any such action shall terminate upon the filing of a complaint by the Secretary in an action under this subsection in which a recovery is sought of unpaid minimum wages or unpaid overtime compensation under sections 206 and 207 of this title or liquidated or other damages provided by this subsection owing to such employee by an employer liable under the provisions of subsection (b) of this section, unless such action is dismissed without prejudice on motion of the Secretary. Any sums thus recovered by the Secretary of Labor on behalf of an employee pursuant to this subsection shall be held in a special deposit account and shall be paid, on order of the Secretary of Labor, directly to the employee or employees affected. Any such sums not paid to an employee because of inability to do so within a period of three years shall be covered into the Treasury of the United States as miscellaneous receipts. In determining when an action is commenced by the Secretary of Labor under this subsection for the purposes of the statutes of limitations provided in section 255(a) of this title, it shall be considered to be commenced in the case of any individual claimant on the date when the complaint is filed if he is specifically named as a party plaintiff in the complaint, or if his name did not so appear, on the subsequent date on which his name is added as a party plaintiff in such action.

* * *

§ 217. Injunction proceedings

The district courts, together with the United States District Court for the District of the Canal Zone, the District Court of the Virgin Islands, and the District Court of Guam shall have jurisdiction, for cause shown, to restrain violations of section 215 of this title, including in the case of violations of section 215(a)(2) of this title the restraint of any withholding of payment of minimum wages or overtime compensation found by the court to be due to employees under this chapter (except sums which employees are barred from recovering, at the time of the commencement of the action to restrain the violations, by virtue of the provisions of section 255 of this title).

* * *

§ 255.   Statute of limitations

Any action commenced on or after May 14, 1947, to enforce any cause of action for unpaid minimum wages, unpaid overtime compensation, or liquidated damages, under the Fair Labor Standards Act of 1938, as amended [29 U.S.C.A. § 201 et seq.], the Walsh–Healey Act [41 U.S.C.A. § 35 et seq.], or the Bacon–Davis Act [40 U.S.C.A. § 276a et seq.]—

(a) if the cause of action accrues on or after May 14, 1947—may be commenced within two years after the cause of action accrued, and every such action shall be forever barred unless commenced within two years after the cause of action accrued, except that a cause of action arising out of a willful violation may be commenced within three years after the cause of action accrued;

* * *

§ 259.   Reliance in future on administrative rulings, etc.

(a) In any action or proceeding based on any act or omission on or after May 14, 1947, no employer shall be subject to any liability or punishment for or on account of the failure of the employer to pay minimum wages or overtime compensation under the Fair Labor Standards Act of 1938, as amended [29 U.S.C.A. § 201 et seq.], the Walsh–Healey Act [41 U.S.C.A. § 35 et seq.], or the Bacon–Davis Act [40 U.S.C.A. § 276a et seq.], if he pleads and proves that the act or omission complained of was in good faith in conformity with and in reliance on any written administrative regulation, order, ruling, approval, or interpretation, of the [DOL or EEOC] section, or any administrative practice or enforcement policy of such agency with respect to the class of employers to which he belonged. Such a defense, if established, shall be a bar to the action or proceeding, notwithstanding that after such act or omission, such administrative regulation, order, ruling, approval, interpretation, practice, or enforcement policy is modified or rescinded or is determined by judicial authority to be invalid or of no legal effect.

* * *

§ 260.   Liquidated damages

In any action commenced prior to or on or after May 14, 1947 to recover unpaid minimum wages, unpaid overtime compensation, or liquidated damages, under the Fair Labor Standards Act of 1938, as amended [29 U.S.C.A. § 201 et seq.], if the employer shows to the satisfaction of the court that the act or omission giving rise to such action was in good faith and that he had reasonable grounds for believing that his act or omission was not a violation of the Fair Labor Standards Act of 1938, as amended, the court may, in its sound discretion, award no liquidated damages or award any amount thereof not to exceed the amount specified in section 216 of this title.

THE IMMIGRATION REFORM AND CONTROL ACT OF 1986

100 Stat. 3359, P.L. 99–603, § 102, 8 U.S.C.A. § 1324B

[This Act addressed various aspects of immigration law, including a prohibition on employing illegal immigrants. The excerpts below address practices that are prohibited employment discrimination.]

§ 102.   Unfair Immigration–Related Employment Practices.

(a) Prohibition of Discrimination Based on National Origin or Citizenship Status.—

(1) General Rule.—It is an unfair immigration-related employment practice for a person or other entity to discriminate against any individual (other than an unauthorized alien) with respect to the hiring, or recruitment or referral for a fee, of the individual for employment or the discharging of the individual from employment—

(A) because of such individual's national origin, or

(B) in the case of a citizen or intending citizen (as defined in paragraph (3)), because of such individual's citizenship status.

(2) Exceptions.—Paragraph (1) shall not apply to—

(A) a person or other entity that employs three or fewer employees,

(B) a person's or entity's discrimination because of an individual's national origin if the discrimination with respect to that person or entity and that individual is covered under section 703 of the Civil Rights Act of 1964, or

(C) discrimination because of citizenship status which is otherwise required in order to comply with law, regulation, or executive order, or required by Federal, State, or local government contract, or which the Attorney General determines to be essential for an employer to do business with an agency or department of the Federal, State, or local government.

(3) Definition of citizen or intending citizen.—As used in paragraph (1), the term "citizen or intending citizen' means an individual who—

(A) is a citizen or national of the United States, or

(B) is an alien who—

(i) is lawfully admitted for permanent residence, is granted the status of an alien lawfully admitted for temporary residence under section 245A(a)(1), is admitted as a refugee under section 207, or is granted asylum under section 208, and

(ii) evidences an intention to become a citizen of the United States through completing a declaration of intention to become a citizen;

but does not include (I) an alien who fails to apply for naturalization within six months of the date the alien first becomes eligible (by virtue of period of lawful permanent residence) to apply for naturalization or, if later, within six months after the date of the enactment of this section and (II) an alien who has applied on a timely basis, but has not been naturalized as a citizen within 2 years after the date of the application, unless the alien can establish that the alien is actively pursuing naturalization, except that time consumed in the Service's processing the application shall not be counted toward the 2-year period.

(4) Additional exception providing right to prefer equally qualified citizens.—Notwithstanding any other provision of this section, it is not an unfair immigration-related employment practice for a person or other entity to prefer to hire, recruit, or refer an individual who is a citizen or national of the United States over another individual who is an alien if the two individuals are equally qualified.

(b) Charges of Violations.—

(1) In general.—Except as provided in paragraph (2), any person alleging that the person is adversely affected directly by an unfair immigration-related employment practice (or a person on that person's behalf) or an officer of the Service alleging that an unfair immigration-related employment practice has occurred or is occurring may file a charge respecting such practice or violation with the Special Counsel (appointed under subsection (c)). Charges shall be in writing under oath or affirmation and shall contain such information as the Attorney General requires. The Special Counsel by certified mail shall serve a notice of the charge (including the date, place, and circumstances of the alleged unfair immigration-related employment practice) on the person or entity involved within 10 days.

(2) No overlap with EEOC complaints.—No charge may be filed respecting an unfair immigration-related employment practice described in subsection (a)(1)(A) if a charge with respect to that practice based on the same set of facts has been filed with the Equal Employment Opportunity Commission under title VII of the Civil Rights Act of 1964, unless the charge is dismissed as being outside the scope of such title. No charge respecting an employment practice may be filed with the Equal Employment Opportunity Commission under such title if a charge with respect to such practice based on the same set of facts has been filed under this subsection, unless the charge is dismissed under this section as being outside the scope of this section.

(c) Special Counsel—

(1) Appointment.—The President shall appoint, by and with the advice and consent of the Senate, a Special Counsel for Immigration–Related Unfair Employment Practices (hereinafter in this section referred to as the "Special Counsel") within the Department of Justice to serve for a term of four years. In the case of a vacancy in the office of the

Special Counsel the President may designate the officer or employee who shall act as Special Counsel during such vacancy.

(2) Duties.—The Special Counsel shall be responsible for investigation of charges and issuance of complaints under this section and in respect of the prosecution of all such complaints before administrative law judges and the exercise of certain functions under subsection (j)(1).

(3) Compensation.—The Special Counsel is entitled to receive compensation at a rate not to exceed the rate now or hereafter provided for grade GS–17 of the General Schedule, under section 5332 of title 5, United States Code.

(4) Regional offices.—The Special Counsel, in accordance with regulations of the Attorney General, shall establish such regional offices as may be necessary to carry out his duties.

(d) Investigation of Charges—

(1) By special counsel.—The Special Counsel shall investigate each charge received and, within 120 days of the date of the receipt of the charge, determine whether or not there is reasonable cause to believe that the charge is true and whether or not to bring a complaint with respect to the charge before an administrative law judge. The Special Counsel may, on his own initiative, conduct investigations respecting unfair immigration-related employment practices and, based on such an investigation and subject to paragraph (3), file a complaint before such a judge.

(2) Private actions.—If the Special Counsel, after receiving such a charge respecting an unfair immigration-related employment practice which alleges knowing and intentional discriminatory activity or a pattern or practice of discriminatory activity, has not filed a complaint before an administrative law judge with respect to such charge within such 120-day period, the person making the charge may (subject to paragraph (3)) file a complaint directly before such a judge.

(3) Time limitations on complaints.—No complaint may be filed respecting any unfair immigration-related employment practice occurring more than 180 days prior to the date of the filing of the charge with the Special Counsel. This subparagraph shall not prevent the subsequent amending of a charge or complaint under subsection (e)(1).

(e) Hearing.—

(1) Notice.—Whenever a complaint is made that a person or entity has engaged in or is engaging in any such unfair immigration-related employment practice, an administrative law judge shall have power to issue and cause to be served upon such person or entity a copy of the complaint and a notice of hearing before the judge at a place therein fixed, not less than five days after the serving of the complaint. Any such complaint may be amended by the judge conducting the hearing, upon the motion of the party filing the complaint, in the judge's discretion at any time prior to the issuance of an order based thereon. The person or entity so complained of shall have the right to file an answer to the

original or amended complaint and to appear in person or otherwise and give testimony at the place and time fixed in the complaint.

(2) Judges hearing cases.—Hearings on complaints under this subsection shall be considered before administrative law judges who are specially designated by the Attorney General as having special training respecting employment discrimination and, to the extent practicable, before such judges who only consider cases under this section.

(3) Complainant as party.—Any person filing a charge with the Special Counsel respecting an unfair immigration-related employment practice shall be considered a party to any complaint before an administrative law judge respecting such practice and any subsequent appeal respecting that complaint. In the discretion of the judge conducting the hearing, any other person may be allowed to intervene in the said proceeding and to present testimony.

(f) Testimony and Authority of Hearing Officer.—

(1) Testimony.—The testimony taken by the administrative law judge shall be reduced to writing. Thereafter, the judge, in his discretion, upon notice may provide for the taking of further testimony or hear argument.

(2) Authority of administrative law judges.—In conducting investigations and hearings under this subsection and in accordance with regulations of the Attorney General, the Special Counsel and administrative law judges shall have reasonable access to examine evidence of any person or entity being investigated. The administrative law judges by subpoena may compel the attendance of witnesses and the production of evidence at any designated place or hearing. In case of contumacy or refusal to obey a subpoena lawfully issued under this paragraph and upon application of the administrative law judge, an appropriate district court of the United States may issue an order requiring compliance with such subpoena and any failure to obey such order may be punished by such court as a contempt thereof.

(g) Determinations.—

(1) Order.—The administrative law judge shall issue and cause to be served on the parties to the proceeding an order, which shall be final unless appealed as provided under subsection (i).

(2) Orders finding violations.—

(A) In general.—If, upon the preponderance of the evidence, an administrative law judge determines that any person or entity named in the complaint has engaged in or is engaging in any such unfair immigration-related employment practice, then the judge shall state his findings of fact and shall issue and cause to be served on such person or entity an order which requires such person or entity to cease and desist from such unfair immigration-related employment practice.

(B) Contents of order.—Such an order also may require the person or entity—

(i) to comply with the requirements of section 274A(b) with respect to individuals hired (or recruited or referred for employment for a fee) during a period of up to three years;

(ii) to retain for the period referred to in clause (i) and only for purposes consistent with section 274(b)(5), the name and address of each individual who applies, in person or in writing, for hiring for an existing position, or for recruiting or referring for a fee, for employment in the United States;

(iii) to hire individuals directly and adversely affected, with or without back pay; and

(iv)(I) except as provided in subclause (II), to pay a civil penalty of not more than $1,000 for each individual discriminated against, and

(II) in the case of a person or entity previously subject to such an order, to pay a civil penalty of not more than $2,000 for each individual discriminated against.

(C) Limitation on back pay remedy.—In providing a remedy under subparagraph (B)(iii), back pay liability shall not accrue from a date more than two years prior to the date of the filing of a charge with an administrative law judge. Interim earnings or amounts earnable with reasonable diligence by the individual or individuals discriminated against shall operate to reduce the back pay otherwise allowable under such subparagraph. No order shall require the hiring of an individual as an employee or the payment to an individual of any back pay, if the individual was refused employment for any reason other than discrimination on account of national origin or citizenship status.

(D) Treatment of distinct entities.—In applying this subsection in the case of a person or entity composed of distinct, physicially separate subdivisions each of which provides separately for the hiring, recruiting, or referring for employment, without reference to the practices of, and not under the control of or common control with, another subdivision, each such subdivision shall be considered a separate person or entity.

(3) Orders not finding violations.—If upon the preponderance of the evidence an administrative law judge determines that the person or entity named in the complaint has not engaged or is not engaging in any such unfair immigration-related employment practice, then the judge shall state his findings of fact and shall issue an order dismissing the complaint.

(h) Awarding of Attorneys' Fees.—

In any complaint respecting an unfair immigration-related employment practice, an administrative law judge, in the judge's discretion, may allow a prevailing party, other than the United States, a reasonable attorney's fee, if the losing party's argument is without reasonable foundation in law and fact.

(i) Review of Final Orders.—

(1) In general.—Not later than 60 days after the entry of such final order, any person aggrieved by such final order may seek a review of such order in the United States court of appeals for the circuit in which the violation is alleged to have occurred or in which the employer resides or transacts business.

(2) Further review.—Upon the filing of the record with the court, the jurisdiction of the court shall be exclusive and its judgment shall be final, except that the same shall be subject to review by the Supreme Court of the United States upon writ of certiorari or certification as provided in section 1254 of title 28, United States Code.

(j) Court Enforcement of Administrative Orders.—

(1) In general.—If an order of the agency is not appealed under subsection (i)(1), the Special Counsel (or, if the Special Counsel fails to act, the person filing the charge) may petition the United States district court for the district in which a violation of the order is alleged to have occurred, or in which the respondent resides or transacts business, for the enforcement of the order of the administrative law judge, by filing in such court a written petition praying that such order be enforced.

(2) Court enforcement order.—Upon the filing of such petition, the court shall have jurisdiction to make and enter a decree enforcing the order of the administrative law judge. In such a proceeding, the order of the administrative law judge shall not be subject to review.

(3) Enforcement decree in original review.—If, upon appeal of an order under subsection (i)(1), the United States court of appeals does not reverse such order, such court shall have the jurisdiction to make and enter a decree enforcing the order of the administrative law judge.

(4) Awarding of attorney's fees.—In any judicial proceeding under subsection (i) or this subsection, the court, in its discretion, may allow a prevailing party, other than the United States, a reasonable attorney's fee as part of costs but only if the losing party's argument is without reasonable foundation in law and fact.

(k) Termination Dates.—

(1) This section shall not apply to discrimination in hiring, recruiting, referring, or discharging of individuals occurring after the date of any termination of the provisions of section 274A, under subsection (*l*) or that section.

(2) The provisions of this section shall terminate 30 calendar days after receipt of the last report required to be transmitted under section 274A(j) if—

(A) the Comptroller General determines, and so reports in such report that—

(i) no significant discrimination has resulted, against citizens or nationals of the United States or against any eligible workers seeking employment, from the implementation of section 274A, or

(ii) such section has created an unreasonable burden on employers hiring such workers; and

(B) there has been enacted, within such period of 30 calendar days, a joint resolution stating in substance that the Congress approves the findings of the Comptroller General contained in such report.

The provisions of subsections (m) and (n) of section 274A shall apply to any joint resolution under subparagraph (B) in the same manner as they apply to a joint resolution under subsection (*l*) of such section.

* * *

CIVIL RIGHTS ATTORNEYS' FEES
AWARDS ACT OF 1976

(42 U.S.C.A. § 1988)

§ 1988. Proceedings in vindication of civil rights; attorney's fees

* * *

In any action or proceeding to enforce a provision of sections 1981, 1982, 1983, 1985, and 1986 of this title, title IX of Public Law 92–318, or title VI of the Civil Rights Act of 1964, the court, in its discretion, may allow the prevailing party, other than the United States, a reasonable attorney's fee as part of the costs.

FAMILY AND MEDICAL LEAVE ACT OF 1993

107 Stat. 6 (1993), as amended 109 Stat. 3 (1995)

§ 2601.   Findings and Purposes (§ 2)

(a) Findings

Congress finds that—

(1) the number of single-parent households and two-parent households in which the single parent or both parents work is increasing significantly;

(2) it is important for the development of children and the family unit that fathers and mothers be able to participate in early childrearing and the care of family members who have serious health conditions;

(3) the lack of employment policies to accommodate working parents can force individuals to choose between job security and parenting;

(4) there is inadequate job security for employees who have serious health conditions that prevent them from working for temporary periods;

(5) due to the nature of the roles of men and women in our society, the primary responsibility for family caretaking often falls on women, and such responsibility affects the working lives of women more than it affects the working lives of men; and

(6) employment standards that apply to one gender only have serious potential for encouraging employers to discriminate against employees and applicants for employment who are of that gender.

(b) Purposes.

It is the purpose of this Act—

(1) to balance the demands of the workplace with the needs of families, to promote the stability and economic security of families, and to promote national interests in preserving family integrity;

(2) to entitle employees to take reasonable leave for medical reasons, for the birth or adoption of a child, and for the care of a child, spouse, or parent who has a serious health condition;

(3) to accomplish the purposes described in paragraphs (1) and (2) in a manner that accommodates the legitimate interests of employers;

(4) to accomplish the purposes described in paragraphs (1) and (2) in a manner that, consistent with the Equal Protection Clause of the Fourteenth Amendment, minimizes the potential for employment discrimination on the basis of sex by ensuring generally that leave is available for eligible medical reasons (including maternity-related disability) and for compelling family reasons, on a gender-neutral basis; and

(5) to promote the goal of equal employment opportunity for women and men, pursuant to such clause.

§ 2611.   Definitions (§ 101)

As used in this title:

(1) Commerce.—The terms "commerce" and "industry or activity affecting commerce" means any activity, business, or industry in commerce or in which a labor dispute would hinder or obstruct commerce or the free flow of commerce, and include "commerce" and any "industry affecting commerce", as defined in paragraphs (1) and (3) of section 501 of the Labor Management Relations Act, 1947 (29 U.S.C. 142(1) and (3)).

(2) Eligible Employee—

(A) In General.—The term "eligible employee" means an employee who has been employed—

(i) for at least 12 months by the employer with respect to whom leave is requested under section 102; and

(ii) for at least 1,250 hours of service with such employer during the previous 12-month period.

(B) Exclusions.—The term "eligible employee" does not include—

(i) any Federal officer or employee covered under subchapter V of chapter 63 of title 5, United States Code (as added by title II of this Act); or

(ii) any employee of an employer who is employed at a worksite at which such employer employs less than 50 employees if the total number of employees employed by that employer within 75 miles of that worksite is less than 50.

(C) Determination.—For purposes of determining whether an employee meets the hours of service requirement specified in subparagraph (A)(ii), the legal standards established under section 7 of the Fair Labor Standards Act of 1938 (29 U.S.C. 207) shall apply.

(3) Employ; Employee; State.—The terms "employ", "employee", and "State" have the same meanings given such terms in subsections (c), (e), and (g) of section 3 of the Fair Labor Standards Act of 1938 (29 U.S.C. 203(c), (e), and (g)).

(4) Employer.—

(A) In General.—The term "employer"—

(i) means any person engaged in commerce or in any industry or activity affecting commerce who employs 50 or more employees for each working day during each of 20 or more calendar workweeks in the current or preceding calendar year;

(ii) includes—

(I) any person who acts, directly or indirectly, in the interest of an employer to any of the employees of such employer;

(II) any successor in interest of an employer;

(iii) includes any "public agency", as defined in section 3(x) of the Fair Labor Standards Act of 1938 (29 U.S.C. 203(x)), and

(iv) includes the General Accounting Office and the Library of Congress. [effective Jan. 23, 1996—Eds.]

(B) Public Agency.—For purposes of subparagraph (A)(iii), a public agency shall be considered to be a person engaged in commerce or in an industry or activity affecting commerce.

(5) Employment Benefits. The term "employment benefits" means all benefits provided or made available to employees by an employer, including group life insurance, health insurance, disability insurance, sick leave, annual leave, educational benefits, and pensions, regardless of whether such benefits are provided by a practice or written policy of an employer or through an "employee benefit plan", as defined in section 3(3) of the Employee Retirement Income Security Act of 1974 (29 U.S.C. 1002(3)).

(6) Health Care Provider.—The term "health care provider" means—

(A) a doctor of medicine or osteopathy who is authorized to practice medicine or surgery (as appropriate) by the State in which the doctor practices; or

(B) any other person determined by the Secretary to be capable of providing health care services.

(7) Parent.—The term "parent" means the biological parent of an employee or an individual who stood in loco parentis to an employee when the employee was a son or daughter.

(8) Person.—The term "person" has the same meaning given such term in section 3(a) of the Fair Labor Standards Act of 1938 (29 U.S.C. 203(a)).

(9) Reduced Leave Schedule.—The term "reduced leave schedule" means a leave schedule that reduces the usual number of hours per workweek, or hours per workday, of an employee.

(10) Secretary.—The term "Secretary" means the Secretary of Labor.

(11) Serious Health Condition.—The term "serious health condition" means an illness, injury, impairment, or physical or mental condition that involves—

(A) inpatient care in a hospital, hospice, or residential medical care facility; or

(B) continuing treatment by a health care provider.

(12) Son or Daughter.—The term "son or daughter" means a biological, adopted, or foster child, a stepchild, a legal ward, or a child of a person standing in loco parentis, who is—

(A) under 18 years of age; or

(B) 18 years of age or older and incapable of self-care because of a mental or physical disability.

(13) Spouse.—The term "spouse" means a husband or wife, as the case may be.

§ 2612.   Leave Requirement (§ 102)

(a) In General.—

(1) Entitlement to Leave.—Subject to section 103, an eligible employee shall be entitled to a total of 12 workweeks of leave during any 12-month period for one or more of the following:

(A) Because of the birth of a son or daughter of the employee and in order to care for such son or daughter.

(B) Because of the placement of a son or daughter with the employee for adoption or foster care.

(C) In order to care for the spouse, or a son, daughter, or parent, of the employee, if such spouse, son, daughter, or parent has a serious health condition.

(D) Because of a serious health condition that makes the employee unable to perform the functions of the position of such employee.

(2) Expiration of Entitlement.—The entitlement to leave under subparagraphs (A) and (B) of paragraph (1) for a birth or placement of a son or daughter shall expire at the end of the 12-month period beginning on the date of such birth or placement.

(b) Leave Taken Intermittently or on a Reduced Leave Schedule.—

(1) In General.—Leave under subparagraph (A) or (B) of subsection (a)(1) shall not be taken by an employee intermittently or on a reduced leave schedule unless the employee and the employer of the employee agree otherwise. Subject to paragraph (2), subsection (e)(2), and section 103(b)(5), leave under subparagraph (C) or (D) of subsection (a)(1) may be taken intermittently or on a reduced leave schedule when medically necessary. The taking of leave intermittently or on a reduced leave schedule pursuant to this paragraph shall not result in a reduction in the total amount of leave to which the employee is entitled under subsection (a) beyond the amount of leave actually taken.

(2) Alternative Position.—If an employee requests intermittent leave, or leave on a reduced leave schedule, under subparagraph (C) or (D) of subsection (a)(1), that is foreseeable based on planned medical treatment, the employer may require such employee to transfer temporarily to an available alternative position offered by the employer for which the employee is qualified and that—

(A) has equivalent pay and benefits; and

(B) better accommodates recurring periods of leave than the regular employment position of the employee.

(c) Unpaid Leave Permitted.

Except as provided in subsection (d), leave granted under subsection (a) may consist of unpaid leave. Where an employee is otherwise exempt under regulations issued by the Secretary pursuant to section 13(a)(1) of the Fair Labor Standards Act of 1938 (29 U.S.C. 213(a)(1)), the compliance of an employer with this title by providing unpaid leave shall not affect the exempt status of the employee under such section.

(d) Relationship to Paid Leave.

(1) Unpaid Leave.—If an employer provides paid leave for fewer than 12 workweeks, the additional weeks of leave necessary to attain the 12 workweeks of leave required under this title may be provided without compensation.

(2) Substitution of Paid Leave.—

(A) In General.—An eligible employee may elect, or an employer may require the employee, to substitute any of the accrued paid vacation leave, personal leave, or family leave of the employee for leave provided under subparagraph (A), (B), or (C) of subsection (a)(1) for any part of the 12-week period of such leave under such subsection.

(B) Serious Health Condition.—An eligible employee may elect, or an employer may require the employee, to substitute any of the accrued paid vacation leave, personal leave, or medical or sick leave of the employee for leave provided under subparagraph (C) or (D) of subsection (a)(1) for any part of the 12-week period of such leave under such subsection, except that nothing in this title shall require an employer to provide paid sick leave or paid medical leave in any situation in which such employer would not normally provide any such paid leave

(e) Foreseeable Leave.

(1) Requirement of Notice.—In any case in which the necessity for leave under subparagraph (A) or (B) of subsection (a)(1) is foreseeable based on an expected birth or placement, the employee shall provide the employer with not less than 30 days' notice, before the date the leave is to begin, of the employee's intention to take leave under such subparagraph, except that if the date of the birth or placement requires leave to begin in less than 30 days, the employee shall provide such notice as is practicable.

(2) Duties of Employee.—In any case in which the necessity for leave under subparagraph (C) or (D) of subsection (a)(1) is foreseeable based on planned medical treatment, the employee—

(A) shall make a reasonable effort to schedule the treatment so as not to disrupt unduly the operations of the employer, subject to the approval of the health care provider of the employee or the health care provider of the son, daughter, spouse, or parent of the employee, as appropriate; and

(B) shall provide the employer with not less than 30 days' notice, before the date the leave is to begin, of the employee's intention to take leave under such subparagraph, except that if the date of the treatment requires leave to begin in less than 30 days, the employee shall provide such notice as is practicable.

(f) Spouses Employed by the Same Employer.

In any case in which a husband and wife entitled to leave under subsection (a) are employed by the same employer, the aggregate number of workweeks of leave to which both may be entitled may be limited to 12 workweeks during any 12-month period, if such leave is taken—

(1) under subparagraph (A) or (B) of subsection (a)(1); or

(2) to care for a sick parent under subparagraph (C) of such subsection.

* * *

§ 2614.   Employment and Benefits Protection (§ 104)

(a) Restoration to Position.

(1) In General.—Except as provided in subsection (b), any eligible employee who takes leave under section 102 for the intended purpose of the leave shall be entitled, on return from such leave—

(A) to be restored by the employer to the position of employment held by the employee when the leave commenced; or

(B) to be restored to an equivalent position with equivalent employment benefits, pay, and other terms and conditions of employment.

(2) Loss of Benefits.—The taking of leave under section 102 shall not result in the loss of any employment benefit accrued prior to the date on which the leave commenced.

(3) Limitations.—Nothing in this section shall be construed to entitle any restored employee to—

(A) the accrual of any seniority or employment benefits during any period of leave; or

(B) any right, benefit, or position of employment other than any right, benefit, or position to which the employee would have been entitled had the employee not taken the leave.

* * *

§ 2615.   Prohibited Acts (§ 105)

(a) Interference with Rights.

(1) Exercise of Rights.—It shall be unlawful for any employer to interfere with, restrain, or deny the exercise of or the attempt to exercise, any right provided under this title.

(2) Discrimination.—It shall be unlawful for any employer to discharge or in any other manner discriminate against any individual for opposing any practice made unlawful by this title.

(b) Interference with Proceedings or Inquiries.

It shall be unlawful for any person to discharge or in any other manner discriminate against any individual because such individual—

(1) has filed any charge, or has instituted or caused to be instituted any proceeding, under or related to this title;

(2) has given, or is about to give, any information in connection with any inquiry or proceeding relating to any right provided under this title; or

(3) has testified, or is about to testify, in any inquiry or proceeding relating to any right provided under this title.

§ 2616. Investigative Authority (§ 106)

(a) In General.

To ensure compliance with the provisions of this title, or any regulation or order issued under this title, the Secretary shall have, subject to subsection (c), the investigative authority provided under section 11(a) of the Fair Labor Standards Act of 1938 (29 U.S.C. 211(a)).

(b) Obligation to Keep and Preserve Records.

Any employer shall make, keep, and preserve records pertaining to compliance with this title in accordance with section 11(c) of the Fair Labor Standards Act of 1938 (29 U.S.C. 211(c)) and in accordance with regulations issued by the Secretary.

(c) Required Submissions Generally Limited to an Annual Basis.

The Secretary shall not under the authority of this section require any employer or any plan, fund, or program to submit to the Secretary any books or records more than once during any 12-month period, unless the Secretary has reasonable cause to believe there may exist a violation of this title or any regulation or order issued pursuant to this title, or is investigating a charge pursuant to section 107(b).

(d) Subpoena Powers.

For the purposes of any investigation provided for in this section, the Secretary shall have the subpoena authority provided for under section 9 of the Fair Labor Standards Act of 1938 (29 U.S.C. 209).

§ 2617. Enforcement (§ 107)

(a) Civil Action by Employees.

(1) Liability.—Any employer who violates section 105 shall be liable to any eligible employee affected—

(A) for damages equal to—

(i) the amount of—

(I) any wages, salary, employment benefits, or other compensation denied or lost to such employee by reason of the violation; or

(II) in a case in which wages, salary, employment benefits, or other compensation have not been denied or lost to the employee, any actual monetary losses sustained by the employee as a direct result of the violation, such as the cost of providing care, up to a sum equal to 12 weeks of wages or salary for the employee;

(ii) the interest on the amount described in clause (i) calculated at the prevailing rate; and

(iii) an additional amount as liquidated damages equal to the sum of the amount described in clause (i) and the interest described in clause (ii), except that if an employer who has violated section 105 proves to the satisfaction of the court that the act or omission which violated section 105 was in good faith and that the employer had reasonable grounds for believing that the act or omission was not a violation of section 105, such court may, in the discretion of the court, reduce the amount of the liability to the amount and interest determined under clauses (i) and (ii), respectively; and

(B) for such equitable relief as may be appropriate, including employment, reinstatement, and promotion.

(2) Right of Action.—An action to recover the damages or equitable relief prescribed in paragraph (1) may be maintained against any employer (including a public agency) in any Federal or State court of competent jurisdiction by any one or more employees for and in behalf of—

(A) the employees; or

(B) the employees and other employees similarly situated.

(3) Fees and Costs.—The court in such an action shall, in addition to any judgment awarded to the plaintiff, allow a reasonable attorney's fee, reasonable expert witness fees, and other costs of the action to be paid by the defendant.

(4) Limitations.—The right provided by paragraph (2) to bring an action by or on behalf of any employee shall terminate—

(A) on the filing of a complaint by the Secretary in an action under subsection (d) in which restraint is sought of any further delay in the payment of the amount described in paragraph (1)(A) to such employee by an employer responsible under paragraph (1) for the payment; or

(B) on the filing of a complaint by the Secretary in an action under subsection (b) in which a recovery is sought of the damages described in paragraph (1)(A) owing to an eligible employee by an employer liable under paragraph (1),

unless the action described in subparagraph (A) or (B) is dismissed without prejudice on motion of the Secretary.

(b) Action by the Secretary.

(1) Administrative Action.—The Secretary shall receive, investigate, and attempt to resolve complaints of violations of section 105 in the same manner that the Secretary receives, investigates, and attempts to resolve complaints of violations of sections 6 and 7 of the Fair Labor Standards Act of 1938 (29 U.S.C. 206 and 207).

(2) Civil Action.—The Secretary may bring an action in any court of competent jurisdiction to recover the damages described in subsection (a)(1)(A).

(3) Sums Recovered. Any sums recovered by the Secretary pursuant to paragraph (2) shall be held in a special deposit account and shall be paid, on order of the Secretary, directly to each employee affected. Any such sums not paid to an employee because of inability to do so within a period of 3 years shall be deposited into the Treasury of the United States as miscellaneous receipts.

(c) Limitation.

(1) In General.—Except as provided in paragraph (2), an action may be brought under this section not later than 2 years after the date of the last event constituting the alleged violation for which the action is brought.

(2) Willful Violation.—In the case of such action brought for a willful violation of section 105, such action may be brought within 3 years of the date of the last event constituting the alleged violation for which such action is brought.

(3) Commencement.—In determining when an action is commenced by the Secretary under this section for the purposes of this subsection, it shall be considered to be commenced on the date when the complaint is filed.

(d) Action for Injunction by Secretary.

The district courts of the United States shall have jurisdiction, for cause shown, in an action brought by the Secretary—

(1) to restrain violations of section 105, including the restraint of any withholding of payment of wages, salary, employment benefits, or other compensation, plus interest, found by the court to be due to eligible employees; or

(2) to award such other equitable relief as may be appropriate, including employment, reinstatement, and promotion.

(e) Solicitor of Labor.

The Solicitor of Labor may appear for and represent the Secretary on any litigation brought under this section.

* * *

* * * See 1978 Reorg. Plan No. 1, § 2, eff. Jan. 1, 1979, 43 F.R. 19807, 92 Stat. 3781.

[Power now exercised by the Equal Employment Opportunity Commission]

†